How Women Executives
Succeed

How Women Executives Succeed

LESSONS AND EXPERIENCES FROM THE FEDERAL GOVERNMENT

Danity Little

QUORUM BOOKS
Westport, Connecticut • London

Library of Congress Cataloging-in-Publication Data

Little, Danity.
    How women executives succeed : lessons and experiences from
the federal government / Danity Little.
      p. cm.
    Includes bibliographical references and index.
    ISBN 0–89930–867–8 (alk. paper)
    1. Women government executives—United States. I. Title.
JK721.L58   1994
353.07'4'082—dc20   93–37027

British Library Cataloguing in Publication Data is available.

Library of Congress Catalog Card Number: 93–37027
ISBN: 0–89930–867–8

First published in 1994

Quorum Books, 88 Post Road West, Westport, CT 06881
An imprint of Greenwood Publishing Group, Inc.

Printed in the United States of America

The paper used in this book complies with the Permanent
Paper Standard issued by the National Information Standards
Organization (Z39.48–1984).

10 9 8 7 6 5 4 3 2 1

To **Jerry A. Hanline**,
for bringing balance to my life by giving me fun

To **my parents, Ester** and **Lester Richardson**,
for instilling in me a work ethic and independence

Contents

Illustrations

Preface

If you can dream it, you can do it.

Walt Disney

Through generations, women have dreamed, suffered, worked, planned, waited, struggled, sacrificed, and survived to contribute to the grand design of having an equal part in our society—our democracy. Today a revolution is underway. Women are taking a journey through the ranks of government. Some are making it to their final destination—a journey to the top ranks of management in the public service—the Senior Executive Service (SES). What has made the difference for them in their career progress?

This book, based on a study of 78 federal senior executive women, examines that question. It is the first systematically researched and documented study of women who have broken the "glass ceiling" in the federal government. These women—at some risk to their own careers—have shared their experiences and the lessons learned that made the ceiling open up to them. Great care has been taken to ensure their own words were used to describe their lessons, experiences, and challenges. From their stories—and their stories needed to be told—every woman who aspires to make it to the top can learn and understand what it takes to be an executive leader.

I hope that any woman in the work force, now and in the future, will be able to use this research to make it to the top. From this research, I know each woman will be able to learn what is happening in her own career and to identify where she is in the journey. She will be able to learn the lessons that are required for her to keep moving and to take action to bring her to her destination: the top.

Acknowledgments

Through the courage and support of so many people who care about other women making it to the top, this book is made possible.

I am grateful to the 78 senior executive women who took time from their busy lives to tell their stories so others may learn from their experiences. Their candor in talking about their career development and growth, setbacks, successes, failures, feelings, and beliefs and the generosity with which they gave of their time made this book a reality.

I am also grateful to the Center for Creative Leadership for support and encouragement. I extend to the center special thanks for permission to use their questionnaire, their enthusiasm to replicate their private-sector study on women in the federal government, and the access they gave me to some of the original data important to this research. My heartfelt thanks go to Randall White for his clear thinking, his research methodology, his ideas, and his inspiration to me as I struggled through the data collection and analysis stages of research. He has been a source of strength, support, and friendship.

For the many women in the federal government who encouraged me to write a book so that the research would not just sit on a shelf—Alma Shea, Joan Wrangler, Diane Sutton, Ellen Roderick, Mary Ann Jacob, Jeanne Ramos, Karin Alvarez, Belinda Zamer, and Margaret Patch—I thank you all.

In various stages of writing the manuscript, seven top-notch professionals gave their time and effort to read, edit, and make suggestions for improvements. Each was dedicated to making the book a helpful guide to assist women in breaking through the glass ceiling. They are JoAnn Vaught, Jean Palmer, Mary Ann Ruth, Helga Buerger, Mary Joe Hall, Vivian Havian, and Carol Jorgensen. I thank you all.

Three people deserve special recognition for their contribution in making this book publishable. JoAnn Vaught was a great source of energy and enthusiasm to me. She encouraged me to make this a readable textbook and to create perspectives and opportunities for women to be all they can be. Throughout the research and writing, she was a source of balance for me. Vivian Havian evaluated the manuscript to make sure I kept on track. And Charles Little, a long-time friend and companion, was patient enough to teach me WordPerfect and produce the graphics. I am indebted to him for his support and encouragement through the research phase of this book.

Many other friends in more ways than I can count made this book happen. They gave encouragement when I ran out of time and energy. Others provided continuous inquiry about the research and showed interest in seeing the subject of making it to the top in government in a book format. This interest bolstered me to take action. I extend special thanks to Ron Stupak, Joe Wholey, Barbara Boyd, Mary Belefski, Patrick Sherrin, Heidi Frick, Nancy Gilmore, Judith Lombard, Malcolm Knowles, Warren Schmidt, Jeff Davidson, and Judith Bardwick for their advice and perspective on the subject of women and executive development.

Words cannot express my thanks and appreciation to Roylene Sims, a trusted and reliable friend, who did more than the administrative editing of this book. She gave me two gifts—time and confidence. For this I am deeply grateful. Without her, this book would not have been completed. Another special thanks goes to Marcy Weiner, the acquisitions editor who believed in the book and its value to other women trying to make it to the top.

To everyone mentioned and the many whom I failed to mention, accept my thanks for all your time, insight, suggestions, ideas, and enthusiasm for this book. Without all of you, it would have been an awesome task; with you, it was a great journey of learning and growth for myself and, I hope, for the future of others.

1

Introduction

Alice: Would you tell me, please, which way I ought to go from here?

Cat: That depends a good deal on where you want to get to.

Alice: I don't much care where—,

Cat: Then it doesn't matter which way you go,

Alice: —just so long as I get somewhere,

Cat: Oh, you're sure to do that, if you only walk long enough.

Alice's Adventure in Wonderland[1]

The world is changing so rapidly that many people need to know which way to go and how to get there. There are others who do not care where they go as long as it is somewhere. Still others know what their destination is—they have walked long enough to get there—and they know how they got there. This uncertainty of where to go, how to get there, and what to do is part of this changing world. Contributing to this instability is the fast-paced technology that renders most skills obsolete almost as soon as they are acquired. Is there anything that can stand the test of time? Can people find the road to success? There is no easy and set answer to these questions. Just like Alice in Wonderland, people are discovering that there are many paths to follow, many people to meet, and many things to overcome before the final way out (or up) is achieved.

In both the public and private sectors, men and women are asking questions about how they can cope with these constant changes within their world, how they can lead and manage in such changing and turbulent environments, and how a successful pathway can be plotted to the top of the organization. Women especially are looking for answers to these questions.

Many recent studies in industry and government have been undertaken to answer some of these questions. This book focuses on the federal government as it relates to being an employer of choice. The government has commissioned several studies to show how and what it will look like in the year 2000: *Workforce 2000, Civil Service 2000, Opportunity 2000,* and *Project 2000.* The results confirmed some of the reports done by the Volcker Commission, which showed that the public sector is going through a "quiet crisis."[2] All of these studies suggest that changes must be made in federal government operations—training and development of employees, the recruitment and selection process, procedures for coping with the budget deficit, and means of working within the political arena—so that public service will remain an important employment option.

Many activities designed to bring about this magnitude of change are occurring simultaneously in the public sector:

First, the work force studies are being paid serious attention. The changing demographics of the work force, as more women and minorities find employment, will have an impact on recruitment, selection, training, development, management, and leadership.

Second, the concept of total quality management, reinforced by the Federal Quality Institute and implemented by agencies trained by a Senior Executive Service member, is causing the top hierarchy to realize that business is not as usual.

Third, the combination of the changing work force and the empowerment of people shows that government leaders are realizing that management gurus Warren Bennis, Peter Drucker, and Tom Peters have been right: people are the capital assets of an organization.

Finally, Constance Newman, former director of the Office of Personnel Management (OPM), initiated a task force composed of senior human resources professors, industry managers, consultants, and senior-level administrators in the government to study the training community and its needs and to design an adult education model that would yield well-trained civil servants who could serve the public interests effectively and efficiently. They used as models the Harvard case study method, the Army Leadership school, executive development programs at prominent universities, and the Federal Executive Institute. Discussions emphasized the differences between private-sector and public-sector training, private-sector and public-sector differences and similarities in leading and managing organizations, and the application of learning on the job. In addition to an overall model, an objective was to elevate the training function within OPM and to implement some of the findings of the task force. They initiated a training policy matrix that will eventually cover all employees from new employee orientation through a pathway of technical, supervisory, management, and executive skills.

These four changes share a common thread: all are setting a new direction for the leadership of the federal government. While this process is occurring, the

Workforce 2000 and *Civil Service 2000* reports have been studied in great depth. They concur that the new work force will be more culturally diverse, have more minorities and immigrants, and include more women. The *Civil Service 2000* report concluded that women will compose two-thirds of the new entrants to the labor force—over 200,000 more women entering federal employment—over the next 10 years.[3] According to the study, the federal government will be primarily an employer of women.

The General Accounting Office (GAO) and the OPM studies show that women and minorities are already well represented in the lower grades of federal service but are underrepresented in the higher grades: they represent less than 10 percent of the career Senior Executive Service (SES). In 1990, Newman disseminated information and gave speeches encouraging the departments to increase their representation of women and minorities in the SES. This is not a new initiative. Over the past twenty-five years, the Civil Rights Act of 1964, the Equal Employment Opportunity Act of 1972 and its amendments, and executive orders have been passed asserting and proclaiming that women and minorities should be able to reach their highest potential. Statistics over these years, however, show little improvement in the upper echelons of government (Table 1.1). If this is not a new initiative, then why all the enthusiasm for a new try at improving the number of women in the SES? The answer lies in the timing, the environment of change, the demographics, the attitude shift, and the need for a qualified and competent work force. Everyone seems to be aware of these differences. The question is, How can the goal of placing more women on the top rungs of the ladder in the federal government be achieved?

The question of career development and mobility within the SES cadre provides few answers, because there is limited research on this population. Questions such as how SES women moved up in their careers, what their experiences were, how they learned, or what made them successful have not been explored. Studies have been conducted in the private sector by the Center for Creative Leadership (CCL) to determine the answers to these questions.[4]

Table 1.1
SES Demographics

	July 1979°	**Sept. 1987°°**	**Oct. 1990°°°**
Total	6,836	6,948	7,413
Sex			
Male	6,489 (94.9%)	6,346 (91.3%)	
Female	347 (5.1%)	602 (8.7%)	657 (8.8%)
Noncareer	16.0%	20.8%	

°U.S. Office of Personnel Management, April 1988, Profile of the Senior Executive Service.
°°Ibid.
°°°SES Evaluation/Data Analysis, telephone request, September 1990.

The public sector has little research that determines how executives learn and what experiences help in their career progression.

This book is based on the first systematic research of executive women and tries to answer how they learn and how they made it to the top. It also explores the lessons, experience, and learning linkages between executive women in the public and private sectors. These linkages show few differences in how women make it to the top in government and in industry.

THE VALUE OF KNOWING

The emphasis given to women in *Workforce 2000* and *Civil Service 2000*, the dearth of research on government executive women, and the need to learn about the career progression of women leaders makes it imperative that the experiences, learnings, and career progression of SES career women be discovered and documented. The importance of this knowledge to the federal government's future work force planning cannot be overlooked. The research data explore the learning, the training, the development, the SES selection, the supervisor, manager, and executive experiences, and the future plans of 78 career SES women located in 33 departments throughout the federal government. As women become more prominent in the government and more significant in their roles as managers and leaders, there is a need to know more about how they have learned and developed their skills, how they operate within the government system, and how they became successful and broke the glass ceiling. (The glass ceiling is defined by the Department of Labor as any artificial barrier based on attitudinal or organizational bias that prevents qualified minorities and women from advancing in their organizations into management level positions.) The learning and experiences of these women create a progressive pathway to the top and can be used to design an executive development model that others can integrate into their own career planning. Although there is no best way to a successful career, the research shows there can be anchors of experiences that make the road to the top easier.

The following chapters tell the story of the climb to the executive tower by 78 senior women executives in government. They explore the major issues of learning, people, experiences, leading, balancing life and work, barriers, and career maintenance.

The feelings and the energy of these women have been captured and set out in this book so that other women can capitalize on their experiences in order to make it to the top. The historical foundation is examined in Chapter 2, "Changing Times." It discusses the current research on work force composition, especially the increase in numbers of women. A review of the literature covers areas such as adult learning theories, adult learning models, Havinghurst and Erikson's developmental stages of life, management and leadership theories, SES history, and qualitative research. Each of these areas addresses the role, impact, and history of women. Because of limited federal government research in this area, most of the literature review comes from the private industry, best-selling books, and newspaper accounts. This literature review lays a foundation for understanding the progression of women in the work world. It shows how far women have progressed, generally and specifically, in government. The literature cited shows the learning theories and models that relate to women as learners, executives, and leaders.

Chapter 3, "The Research Question," sets out how this research was designed and the methodology employed to gather the data. It integrates the questionnaire used for this research, which is a modified version of the questionnaire used by the CCL for its studies on private-sector executive women. Readers will be able to answer the same questions and relate them to their own careers.

Chapter 4, "The Learning Domain," presents the premise of the book: women can learn how to climb the ladder to the top. Their lessons are imparted through individual vignettes and anecdotal descriptions.

Chapter 5, "The Experiences," highlights the experiences of these women on their route to the top. A combination of descriptive anecdotes and summary analyses shows the variety, differences, and similarities of experiences and learnings depicted by the 78 women.

Chapter 6, "Getting Help from Others," identifies the main characters who played major roles in the lives of these women. They helped the women to see the route to the top as not only passable but possible. This chapter provides information that shows that mentoring and networking can make a difference.

"Finding the Career," Chapter 7, covers the major occupations, education, and adult developmental stages that made an impact on their career progression. The importance of each of these areas in the career progression of these women is seen through descriptive vignettes.

Chapter 8, "The Woman as a Leader," discusses the transition of women into the world of executives. The emphasis is on characteristics required of women to be leaders and the role of the culture of the workplace in how one succeeds. This chapter also integrates the private-sector studies of executive women leaders.

Chapter 9, "Balance and Barriers," examines the costs and trade-offs of climbing to the top rungs of the executive ladder. It also indicates the need for reassessment of one's career to see if the sacrifices are worth making it to the top. How these executives continue to stay at the top and maintain their reputations is discussed. The barriers are based on the actual experiences of the women. The chapter provides readers with information on the professional and personal barriers that must be overcome before women can progress up the ladder. The question, "What does the future hold for the committed woman executive?" is explored.

Chapter 10, "100 Steps to the Top," concludes the book with recommendations and guidance on climbing the executive ladder based upon the experiences described by the 78 senior executive women who participated in the pioneer effort of career development in the federal government.

These chapters together form a model that can help women move faster up the career ladder, both in government and in industry. The model also can have an impact on the ability of the government to recruit, select, and maintain qualified and competent public service leaders. The findings of the research provide a sound basis by which women can achieve their highest potential. The federal government can attract, develop, and maintain high-quality talent if it chooses to be committed to making opportunities available and using its untapped resources. With a better-prepared work force, a workable executive development model, and an enlightened system of learning, the government could be the employer of choice instead of the employer of last resort.

NOTES

1. Lewis Carroll, *Alice's Adventure in Wonderland and Through the Looking Glass* (Racine, WI: Whitman Publishing Company, 1955), 66.

2. Paul A. Volcker, *Public Service: The Quiet Crisis* (Lanham, MD: UPA for the American Enterprise Institute for Public Policy Research, 1988).

3. William B. Johnston, *Civil Service 2000* (Indianapolis, IN: Hudson Institute, 1988).

4. Morgan W. McCall, Jr., Michael M. Lombardo, and Ann M. Morrison, *The Lessons of Experience: How Successful Executives Develop On the Job* (Lexington, MA: Lexington Books, 1988); Ann Morrison, Randall White, and Ellen Van Velsor, *Breaking the Glass Ceiling: Can Women Reach the Top of America's Largest Corporations?* (Reading, MA: Addison-Wesley, 1987).

2

Changing Times

The literature review associated with learning and with how one acquires the abilities and skills to be an executive encompasses broad areas of human behavior, organizational theory, and adult learning theories. Each topic has been narrowed to cover selected theories related to learning, developmental stages, adult learner, careers, women, and leaders. Specifically, the literature review addresses some of the past and current thinking on adult learning theories, adult learning models, development stages in life, SES history, women's studies, leadership and management theories, and current studies on the changing organization and the changing role of men and women in the workplace.

The core of this study is anchored in the field of learning. The importance of learning is well articulated by Robert Denhardt:

> Theory and practice seem to be connected in the process of personal learning. As individuals live and work in public organizations, as they read and inquire about the work of others in such organizations, they build a body of experience that is extremely valuable for practice. However, until that body of material is analyzed, reflected on, and generalized into theory, it is really not useful for action. To build a theory is to learn a new way of viewing the world; indeed, it is to construct a new reality for our lives and our work. The process of theory building is a process of learning. Therefore, any approach to action in public organizations must encompass not only a theory of organization but a theory of learning as well.[1]

P. Delker also provides insight into adult learning: "Adult learning is a major, continuing model of adult behavior permeating the major categories of human experience and the major sectors of society."[2]

LEARNING

Although much research has gone into the shared understanding of learning—how one learns, where one should learn, when one should learn, and why one learns—there is an emergency in the education system: a need for more qualified people in higher-skilled positions. *Workforce 2000* and other similar studies have indicated that women, minorities, and immigrants will compose 85 percent of the new hires between 1985 and 2000.[3] Moreover, because of changing demographics—a decline in the population of those 18 to 24 years old—there will be a shortage of labor for entry-level jobs. To remain a competitive nation, the United States must incorporate its innovative spirit in finding ways to teach people how to learn.

Learning is an ongoing process throughout one's lifetime to ensure that skills and workers are available to keep up with the changing complexity of the world. Lifelong learning, according to R. Gross, means self-directed growth:

> It means understanding yourself and the world. It means acquiring new skills and powers—the only true wealth which you can never lose. It means investment in yourself. Lifelong learning means the joy of discovering how something really works, the delight of becoming aware of some new beauty in the world, the fun of creating something, alone or with other people.[4]

Learning, developing, and growing are crucial to keeping qualified and competent executives to run the government.

How people learn has taken on significant importance in the workplace, business, and academia. David Kolb explains learning as the "process whereby knowledge is created through the transformation of experience."[5] Recent research by Morgan McCall, Michael Lombardo, and Ann Morrison in *The Lessons of Experience* provides further explanation of the role of experience as a learning mechanism for executives.[6]

ADULT LEARNING THEORIES

Learning theory is not a new concept. William James in 1890 and John Dewey in 1938 believed that knowledge is grounded in experience and that learning is a continuous process offering continuity and security within the world. Today, the world is changing rapidly and people are searching for stability. David Kolb thinks this can be achieved through experiential learning.

Kolb's book, *Experiential Learning*, provides an excellent historical review of learning. He captures the essence of Jean Piaget's, Kurt Lewin's, and John Dewey's frameworks for the application of experiential learning theory and shows "that learning is a social process based on carefully cultivated experience which challenges every precept and concept of what nowadays passes for 'teaching.' "[7] Kolb denies that learning can take place only in a classroom and lecture format; rather, it can also occur in "the workplace, the family, the carpool, the community or wherever we gather to work or play or love."[8]

Experiential learning dates back to the 1890s with James, but it was not embraced by adult educators until after World War II, when the classical pedagogical assumptions and models about learning no longer provided adults with what they needed in a rapidly changing world. Alfred North Whitehead was the first to note that times were changing so rapidly that the facts and figures normally valid for a lifetime were no longer true. Today, the life span of human beings is longer than the validity of the facts they have learned; skills are obsolete within ten years—and in high-tech industries, in less than one year. People must continuously learn new skills to maintain their standard of living.

As demographics change, managers and leaders must learn how to operate in a global environment of multicultural diversity. They must learn how to learn and be provided a theory of self-directed inquiry whereby they can change with the times. An old Chinese proverb says: "Teach a person to fish and you have given him a livelihood." Today's proverb could read: "Teach a person how to learn and adapt to today's changing world, and you will give her a livelihood."

How can learning be taught to people to help them have inquiring minds to cope with the changing times? Michael Harmon suggests that individuals are active and not passive and that they will interact within their environment.[9] His theory (although he calls it a new paradigm) implies that individuals will put meaning into their work and the rest of their lives by taking action based on the experiences they determine are important to them. This concept is no different from Dewey's descriptions of individuals who "fill each episode of experience with the potential for movement, from blind impulse to a life of choice and purpose."[10] Dewey called this concept pragmatism, which he defined as the organizing principle toward a life of purpose and self-development.

Lewin emphasized the dialectic process to integrate experience, concepts, observations, and actions. Piaget called for an adaptation toward a balanced tension between accommodation and assimilation in a world of experiences and events. Even Jung showed how we can learn from experience. According to Jung, individual preferences are predictable. When differences, such as introvert versus extrovert, intuition versus sensation, feeling versus thinking, and judging versus perceiving, are known, experiences can be designed that will assist in understanding relationships between and among people. Jung's typology has been refined by Katharine Briggs and her daughter, Isabel Briggs Myers, into a psychological instrument, the Myers-Briggs Type Indicator, which types personality preference.[11] David Kolb summarizes these concepts: "Learning, the creation of knowledge and meaning, occurs through the active extension and grounding of ideas and experiences in the external world and through internal reflection about the attributes of these experiences and ideas."[12]

Using the lessons of experience to design career objectives and to form a personal career development program can ensure the right opportunities for development and growth to occur. Leona Tyler believes that people create and write their own programs by choosing and then living with the consequences of their choices. E. A. Burtt used the root metaphor to show how an organism can grow to its full potential.[13] Other psychologists, including Abraham Maslow with his hierarchy of needs theory, showed how "this organismic view of development is the basis of modern humanistic developmental psychology."[14] Adult growth and development requires adaptive commitment to the learning process, as well as a new awareness of integration. The challenge is to shape one's own experiences by learning how to integrate them—not by simply observing and accepting experiences as they happen. Experiencing an effective choice of new ways of doing things, according to Carl Rogers, brings an integrative consciousness to how one learns.

In 1961, Cyril O. Houle was the first researcher to focus on the internal process of learning. His book, *The Inquiring Mind*, which discussed a study of adult learners and their motivation, yielded a three-way typology of learners: goal oriented, activity oriented, and learning oriented. His student, Allen Tough, extended the research and found that adults go through a natural sequence of steps when they undertake to learn on their own.

The research of Robert Havinghurst, Erik Erikson, Gail Sheehy, and Daniel Levinson indicate that adults go through definite developmental stages in adulthood. What they learn, how they learn, and the need to learn follow a pattern that corresponds to these developmental stages in life. Timing learning concepts to the appropriate developmental stage can enhance the learner's pace and receptivity to a lifelong learning process.

It was Malcolm Knowles who integrated these concepts into what he termed the andragogical model, based on six assumptions: learners must (1) have a need to know, (2) feel responsible for their own decisions, (3) have more and varied experiences than when they were young (thus, giving the learner a self-identity), (4) "be ready to learn those things they need to know and be able to do in order to cope effectively with their real-life situations," (5) have an "orientation to learning" (they learn better if they can apply the learning to real situations), and (6) be motivated either externally or internally.[15] This self-directive learning process plays an important part in developing "human growth and self-actualization" in the adult learner.[16]

Several human relations theorists believe that learners must develop an understanding of self to be self-directed in learning. Chris Argyris's study of personality development indicated that individuals need to understand and learn about their internal selves. Once they are aware of their own behavior, they can change organizations.[17] Donald Schon and Argyris's theory about single-loop and double-loop learning provides a different perspective on how people learn.[18] Before learning can occur, they say, a person's own espoused theory of "doing" must be consistent with what she actually does. In other words, she must practice what she says she believes. Otherwise, learning has no impact. Smith and Havercamp agree that the learning process incorporates knowing about self and reflecting on experiences.[19] Stephen Brookfield, in *Understanding and Facilitating Adult Learning*, also addresses the issue of reflection and its importance in understanding experiences and meanings within the context of the organization. Donald Schon, in *The Reflective Practitioner*, links the learning process of the learner to the importance of reflection in action and emphasizes the need to have reflection-in-action practitioners. He defines reflection-in-action as

> both a consequence and cause of surprise so when a member of a bureaucracy embarks on a course of reflective practice, allowing himself to experience confusion and uncertainty, subjecting his frame and theories to conscious criticism and change, he may increase his capacity to contribute to significant organizational learning, but he also becomes by the same token, a danger to the stable system of rules and procedures within which he is expected to deliver his technical expertise.[20]

The importance of learning how to look, listen, and question provides new experiences and helps the reflection-in-action practitioner to cope with the uncertainties posed by a turbulent environment. Schon brings a different, reflective thinking and acting perspective on how to learn, how much to learn, and how to be aware of overlearning. This is important in designing learning organizations that foster experimentation and growth, which are both necessary to enable reflection-in-action managers to serve as change agents in their organizations.

Another theory to help frame how executives learn stems from the work of Peter Honey and Alan Mumford on learning styles. They believe each individual has a "best way" to learn and that if she knows how she learns, she will understand herself and be better equipped to increase her growth and development.

Adult learning theories have developed into broader categories covering all areas of human behavior and development. These theories form a foundation and become intertwined in the very fabric of an organization, affecting everyone who comes into contact with it. Moving from learning theories to learning models, R. H. Dave sums it up:

> Lifelong education seeks to view education in its totality. It covers formal, nonformal, and informal patterns of education, and attempts to integrate and articulate all structures and stages of education along the vertical (temporal) and horizontal (spatial) dimensions. It is also characterized by flexibility in time, place, content and techniques of learning and hence calls for self-directed learning, sharing of one's enlightenment with others, and adopting varied learning styles and strategies.[21]

ADULT LEARNING MODELS

Models provide a framework to synthesize information in a workable format. From the many adult learning models available, we will look at three to enable woman executives to anchor their learning and experiences so that they can be planned and strategically implemented.

The first model on what motivates learners—that of Cyril O. Houle—is thirty years old, yet it is still considered the most influential study on adult motivation. From Houle's study, three learner groups emerged: goal-oriented learners wanted to obtain a concrete objective, activity-oriented learners accomplished the learning from the activity itself, and learning-oriented learners were continually open to learning and growing. These three types of learners offer a framework to understand why SES career women are motivated to learn and how others can be motivated to learn.

The second model, that of Allen Tough, is an extension of Houle's. It provides the how of learning. Tough shows, through learning patterns and benefits, that learners want to use their knowledge or skill and consciously decide how to take the kind of action necessary to accomplish the learning activity. He calls this "self-directing learning." His five stages of learning (engage in a learning activity, retain the knowledge or skill, apply the knowledge, gain a material reward, or receive a symbolic reward) correlate with the life stages of experiences. This framework will be useful to identify the learning stages that the SES career women experienced.

The third model, by Patricia Cross, entitled Framework of Characteristics of Adults as Learners (CAL), incorporates some of Houle's and Tough's models. She integrates three personal characteristics (physiological/aging, sociocultural/life phases, psychological/developmental stages) with two situational characteristics (part-time learning versus full-time learning and voluntary learning versus compulsory learning). These five variables summarize directly or indirectly the ingredients that enabled the 78 SES career women to learn the how and the what that were required to break the glass ceiling.

These three models do not include all educational or learning designs. However, they seem the most relevant in finding a framework that explains some of the domains of career progression undertaken by these executive women. Each model offers a distinct advantage to knowing more about how executives learn. These frameworks are used to explain, expand upon, and incorporate the findings from the respondents into a model in which one can identify one's own career needs and requirements to move ahead to the top of an organization.

PUBLIC SERVICE CAREER SYSTEM

There are four main types of personnel systems generally associated with the federal government: political appointees (public officials appointed to their position—they are outside of the civil service system and do not possess tenure);

agency career systems (specific agencies, such as the Federal Bureau of Investigation, Public Health Service, military, and others, that have established their own system of recruitment, development, and structure that emphasizes the individual); collective systems (mostly blue-collar workers represented by unions to bargain with agency); and general civil service (mostly white-collar personnel, both professional and nonprofessional, who have tenure). All of the women in this study were in this last category.

The impetus for the general civil service dates back to 1883 with the Pendleton Act. Through the years various reorganization plans have changed the structure, such as the Civil Service Reform Act of 1978 which established the SES. Generally, all positions are classified and graded to require certain qualifications. The grade structure goes from General Schedule (GS) 1 to General Manager (GM) 15, with the next classification SES. All positions are classified based upon their duties and responsibilities. In most major occupational fields (personnel, budget, administrative, medicine, health, finance, accounting, law, physical science, and engineering) there are set standards; some include examinations, licenses, certification, and degrees that must be job related. In nonprofessional positions (clerical and administrative), employees usually enter in grades GS-1 through GS-7; professional grades usually begin at GS-5. For promotions from one grade to another, each person must stay at least one year for the work experience in that occupation. Each of the grades has ten increments (called within grades) for people to progress through when promotions are not available.

The selection process for any general civil service position consists of most of these steps: vacancy announcement, panel review, testing, interview, and selection. In most positions there is a one-year probationary period: new employee, new supervisor, new manager, and new SES members.

The SES is the highest level within the career system. Each person must meet certain qualification competencies (managerial and technical) before they can be approved by an Office of Personnel Management (OPM) Qualifications Review Board. Within the SES structure, there are six levels, SES 1 through 6. Each level denotes a position that has more breadth, knowledge, skills, and abilities requirements than the previous level. There are many titles, such as agency head, comptroller, director of information resources, head of a research center, financial officer, or human resource director.

THE SENIOR EXECUTIVE SERVICE

The history of the Senior Executive Service is important to an understanding of how one learns within a government environment. This history can be traced from the call for a cadre of career administrators by Leonard White in 1935 to a review of the elite SES corps directed by the recertification act of 1991. In 1935, Leonard White suggested in the Report of the Commission of Inquiry on Public Service Personnel that public employment be "a worth-while life work, with entrance to the service open and attractive to young men and women of capacity and character, and with opportunity of advancement through service and growth to posts of distinction and honor."[22] In 1937, Floyd W. Reeves and Paul T. David recommended that "a corps of career administrators immediately subordinate to policy-forming officials should therefore be regarded as indispensable to the successful functioning of the Executive Branch."[23] Other efforts were initiated for a separate corps of senior administrators. The Second Hoover Commission proposed in 1955 a permanent senior executive corps, to be called the Senior Civil Service, that would adopt the "British system of a highly mobile, administrative class of career generalists."[24] Congress rejected the proposal.

In 1968, during the Johnson administration, changes within the government (executive orders were issued to outlaw sex discrimination, new social programs required more specialists, and specific skills were required in the fields of technology, space, and computers) made it necessary to have training at all levels. To achieve training for the higher-level executives, President Johnson established "a center for advanced study for executives in upper echelons of the Civil Service." That led to the creation of the Federal Executive Institute (FEI), with the mission to "heighten responsiveness to national needs and goals, to increase appreciation of the totality of the governmental systems, and to improve knowledge of managerial processes."[25] At first, the program at FEI was seven weeks long and provided the executives with mind-stretching experiences on a personal and professional level.

During the Nixon administration, a Federal Executive Service was recommended, with renewable three-year contracts, career and noncareer executives, and mobility assignments. These major issues proved controversial, and the creation of a separate executive service was rejected.

In 1978, a reorganization of the magnitude necessary to cause major changes within the government's personnel system was implemented when the Civil Service Commission became the Office of Personnel Management. The work that was started in 1935 became a reality through the Civil Service Reform Act of 1978. A separate personnel system for executives was created, and the Senior Executive Service was established in July 1979. The SES cadre would be one step below the president or Senate-confirmed appointees. Its major objectives are

> to provide greater authority to agencies in managing their executive resources; to attract and retain highly competent executives, and to assign them where they will be most effective in accomplishing the agency's mission and where best use will be made of their talents; to provide for the systematic development of managers and executives; to hold executives accountable for individual and organizational performance; to reward the outstanding performers and remove the poor performers; and to provide for an executive merit system free of prohibited personnel practices and arbitrary actions.[26]

Since its creation in 1978, limited changes within the objectives and mission of the SES have occurred. The pay raise, the recertification law, and a predicted mass exodus of senior executives beginning in 1994 to 1997 have and will continue to have an impact on the entry of women and minorities into the executive cadre. The recertification process requires that executives continue their education, linking performance to pay. Women and minorities have been able to progress into the upper levels of management, however slowly, through their expertise in specialty areas or through the educational process. The discovery of learning the necessary lessons and experiences and the transitional phases in the executives' careers yielded a series of steps that has made a difference. This combination has helped women and minorities climb to the top of the public service career ladder.

ADULT STAGES OF DEVELOPMENT

Adult development is characterized by different life and career stages. There are many adult development models—the major ones are described by Robert Havinghurst, Erik Erikson, Roger Gould, Gail Sheehy, and Daniel Levinson—and very few use women as their research subject. The models all have some overlapping phases, but each represents a different perspective.

Recent research focusing on these various models has led to the realization that there must be a more flexible interpretation of the data. Most of the work was conducted predominantly with males, and thus some of the models do not apply to women. Where in these models does a woman fit who returns to school at age 40 and enters the work force at 45: in Erikson's Intimacy versus Isolation stage or in Gould's Die Is Cast stage? Both psychologists offer explanations that make it plausible for the woman to be in both stages. These models need to be used as guidelines in comparing the executive women's responses to how they learned at different times in their lives.

STUDIES RELATING TO WOMEN AS EXECUTIVES, LEADERS, AND LEARNERS

Numerous studies, books, articles, and stories treat women and their relationship to home, family, children, husband, marriage, and work; few have focused on the woman as a learner, an executive, or a leader. Yet throughout history, women have been contributors to society, shaped America, and exercised their power and their abilities through various interests. The following chronology depicts women who have had an impact by their leadership, their ideas, and their action. (This list stops in 1940 because that is when women began to enter the work force in larger numbers and were recognized as a valuable asset to the country, especially as they moved into nontraditional jobs created by World War II.)

1773   The first woman probably to have worked for the government was Mary K. Goddard, postmaster at Baltimore, Maryland.[27]

1776	Abigail Adams urged John Adams to "Remember the Ladies" when making the laws of the land. In a letter she warned him that the ladies would revolt if they did not have representation. She also supported women's development and the need to have "learned women."[28]
1786	The second woman employed by the federal government was Elizabeth Cresswell, postmaster at Charlestown, Maryland.[29]
1794–96	The first post rider was Anne Blount.[30]
1819	Emma Willard wrote *A Plan for Female Training*, the first book to show the need for education for females.[31]
1829	Frances Wright wrote, "Let women stand where they may in the scale of improvement, their position decides that of the race."[32]
1838	The first woman to address a state legislature was Angelina Grimké.[33]
1840s	Margaret Fuller, a literary genius and the first woman on staff of a New York newspaper, led many women to speak out and voice their own opinions; she knew the power of speech. She brought out the best in people.[34]
	Mrs. Hale did fund raising to preserve Mount Vernon and later was responsible for persuading President Lincoln to establish Thanksgiving Day.[35]
1841	Dorothea L. Dix took up the cause of the insane and spoke before the legislature to get what she needed because she felt it was a public issue. She established the first model asylum in New Jersey, created over 32 hospitals in her lifetime, wrote a prison manual with standards and called for reform in the prisons, and started libraries and workshops for the mentally ill. Dix knew how to cut through paralyzing red tape to secure reform. She was named to fill the first executive post for the government as superintendent of army nurses.[36]
1848	Lucretia Mott and Elizabeth Cady Stanton led a "Woman's Rights Convention" establishing a "Declaration of Principles" declaring "all men and women are created equal."[37]
1849	Elizabeth Blackwell graduated from medical school, and her efforts opened up the medical profession to women. During the Civil War she gathered over 300 women doctors and surgeons to help the Union armies.[38]
1850s	Harriet Beecher Stowe, author of *Uncle Tom's Cabin*, was America's most celebrated author. Lincoln said this book "made the big war."[39]
1854	Three women worked as clerk-copyists in the Patent Office; one was Clara Barton, who had someone substitute for her while she cared for the soldiers in the Civil War. The first females to work in a government building caused quite a stir.[40]
1860s	During the war, many women worked in the federal government, mainly as copyists; some filled cartridge cases with powder in arsenals, and some assisted in the printing of money.[41]
1862	Jennie Douglas was the Department of Treasury's first woman employee hired to cut and trim paper.[42]

1863   Mary Livermore was probably the first procurement officer; she collected food, money, clothes, and supplies for soldiers.[43]

1864   First statutory recognition of women, which established a maximum salary of $600 a year for women clerks.[44]

Anna E. Dickson, the first professional woman lecturer, gave eloquent speeches for the Republican party and the Connecticut Committee. She spoke before a joint session of Congress at a benefit for the Freedmen's Relief Fund.[45]

1868   The Treasury Department experimented with the employment of "ladies" as clerks in the tax offices.[46]

1869   Wyoming Territory gave women the vote due to the efforts of Esther Morris.[47]

1870s   Belva Lockwood "drafted and shepherded through Congress an historic bill granting equal pay for equal work in the federal civil service." She was the first female lawyer to argue in front of the Supreme Court.[48]

1870   Census listed only seven women stenographers in the federal government.

1874   The Department of State hired five women as clerks.[49]

1883   The Civil Service Act of 1883 encouraged women to take examinations. Mary Francis Hoyt, the first woman appointed under the Civil Service Act, worked at the Treasury Department as a clerk, earning $900 a year.[50]

1898   Margaret M. Hanna and Alvey A. Adee during the Spanish-American War coded and decoded messages.[51]

1900s   Florence Kelley changed social history with her concern for children and women in industry. Her work eventually led to the Fair Labor Standards Act.[52]

1909   The first woman to hold a professional or semiprofessional position at the Department of State was Anne H. Shortridge.[53]

1911   Dr. Alice Hamilton was a pioneer in occupational disease and the first woman on the Harvard faculty. Her work and research in the federal government paved the way for the Occupational Disease Act.[54]

1912   Julia Lathrop was named by President Taft to be the head of the Children's Bureau.

1917   Beginning with World War I, women workers were given the opportunity to do nontraditional work. However, very few women were involved in occupations outside the clerical field. Several regulations occurred during this time frame and beyond that had an impact: the enactment of a Civil Service Commission regulation in 1919 that men and women could take examinations; the passage of the Classification Act of 1923 (equal pay for equal work regardless of sex); and the Economy Act of 1932, which discriminated against married women (repealed in 1937).[55]

1931   Jane Addams shared with Nicholas Murray Butler the Nobel Peace Prize for her work in child labor laws, settlement homes, and welfare issues.[56]

1940   "By 1940 approximately one-fourth of all workers in the United States were
            women, but ninety percent were employed as secretaries, typists, and tele-
            phone operators."[57]

Women have participated in the world of work and have always been learners, but they did not receive visibility in the workplace and academia until after
World War II. The war was the turning point; in increasing numbers, women
completed high school, went to college, and chose careers (pink- and blue-collar
jobs), as well as marriage and family. Their presence was felt in both business
and government.

The role of women in the work force—business, academia, government, and
politics—has changed radically since the 1950s. As legislation encouraged
women, they joined the work force, and entered traditional as well as nontraditional careers. Now women students exceed the enrollment of men in law and
business schools and comprise almost 50 percent of the work force. Yet for all of
their progress, they remain underrepresented in top management positions, in
both Fortune 500 companies and the federal government.

The Department of Labor has initiated several studies under the framework
of "the glass ceiling" to discover how women and minorities face subtle discrimination that blocks their rise to the top echelons of management. *Fortune* magazine recently conducted a study of 799 large companies and found that of 4,012
directors, only 19 were women.[58] Although women and minorities compose
nearly a third of middle management of major companies, the percentage of
those in the boardroom is little more than 1 percent. In the government, using
the figures for SES as a comparison for women at the top, career women represent less than 10 percent of the total SES population.[59] These figures are much
higher than in the private sector but nevertheless reflect an underrepresenta-
tion of women in the SES.

To determine how women executives have learned, this book examines
their career progression and their entry into the SES. It is the first study that
has specifically addressed executive development for women at the SES
level. The result was to identify the learnings, events, and lessons that compose the differences and similarities in how SES women manage their careers. Secretary of Labor Elizabeth Dole's statement in 1990 about the
private sector fits the public sector as well: "There can be little doubt that a
woman or minority, no matter how well-schooled, what their wage, or how
thick their portfolio, enters many business organizations with limited or no
hope of reaching the top."[60]

WOMEN AS LEARNERS

Women must learn how to reach the top. One way to discover the route is
to learn how others have progressed: the experiences they were exposed to,
who influenced them, how they broke out of the role of manager into the role

of executive, the transitional stages of movement in their careers, and the role their occupation and environment played. These categories form the essence of the questionnaire/interview that each SES career woman in this research completed.

Specific quantitative research that deals with women as learners in the workplace is limited, yet women represent the fastest-growing segment of the lifelong learning movement, participating in part-time adult learning activities four times faster than their numbers in the population.[61] With the social and technological changes that have accelerated since the 1950s, women have used education to meet their new roles as well as to cope with their traditional roles. Education and experiences have played a major role and had an impact on the career progression of these 78 SES career women.

THE WOMAN EXECUTIVE

Several surveys have studied executive men and women in general categories, such as age, education, marital status, characteristics, skills, intelligence, job satisfaction, and work values. The research completed by the CCL on executive men, described in *Lessons of Experience*, and on executive women, described in *Breaking the Glass Ceiling*, is one of few efforts devoted to learning about the experiences of top executive men and women of Fortune 500 companies. Judith Hoy did a study about learning in the banking industry based on 22 banking women executives.[62] *The Female Advantage*, focusing on interviews with four executive women, demonstrates how women manage and operate in a large corporation and balance the rest of their lives. Very few of these studies address executive women in government and how they have reached the ranks that implement major federal policies. Because of the broad roles that these women play within their positions, they affect every citizen in the United States.

THE WOMAN LEADER

Leadership is an ongoing educational process. It is so vast that it can only be minimally covered here. (Chapter 8 will address on a broader scale the theories and characteristics of a leader and their relationship to how women are leaders.) This book is only a start in the right direction in designing leadership programs for women who are in the public sector.

A leadership direction can be mapped from an examination of the current leadership thinking and its applicability to the career progression of SES women in the public sector. The integration of leadership theories with the answers of the respondents—SES career women—provides insight into the qualities, education, and experience of leaders in the public sector.

THE CHANGING ROLES OF MEN AND WOMEN
IN A CHANGING ORGANIZATION

The roles of both men and women are changing, and they are changing how organizations operate. Even the government, with its reputation as an entrenched bureaucracy, is showing signs of change as its managers confront the budget deficit, the world economy, banking problems, the housing industry, the education crisis, and infrastructures in need of attention. Leaders of today and those of tomorrow must be proactive as they manage these problems.

To keep pace with the present and to anticipate and manage the future, we need to give new meaning to the ways we think, learn, and communicate. Just as Frederick Taylor gave new meaning to work with his scientific management, today's leaders are seeking new ways to describe the information and knowledge revolution and its meaning to work. People are fast becoming the center of an organization. The new form of leadership could be called "heart management," a style of management that embodies the caring and nurturing of promising employees. In addition to the person's competence, an organizational structure must be open to change; it must allow people to make and learn from their mistakes.

These developments constitute a revolution in thinking. They mean changing some fundamental values of how people operate, how organizations are structured, what processes are required, how cultures are developed, and how relationships are converted into teams. Adaption will take time; mind-sets are not easy to change.

The bureaucratic organizations of government are starting to empower their people. They are beginning to treat them as capital assets—nurturing them, listening to their problems, and communicating at different levels. This different method of operating has been recognized and discussed in some best-selling books and articles: Deborah Tannen, *You Just Don't Understand* (1990); Marlene Caroselli, *The Language of Leadership* (1990); Sherry Suib Cohen, *Tender Power* (1989); Judy B. Rosener, "Ways Women Lead," *Harvard Business Review* (November–December 1990); and *Time* magazine, with a special issue, "Women: The Road Ahead," in fall 1990. This literature explores women's roles in organizations as they try to implement some of these new ways of doing business.

The International Women's Forum survey of men and women leaders in 1989 revealed that there may be a transformational or a transitional way to lead in organizations. The path to the top could be wider, nontraditional leadership styles are effective, and an interactive leadership pattern is just as effective as the command and control style. Another important conclusion of the forum's study is that some organizations need leaders who will operate with different styles of management—authoritarian, laissez faire, and participative. Leaders must know when and how to use these management styles in their organizational context. The new style of leadership is being observed and experienced as women move into top management.

THE OUTCOME

The research literature is limited as it relates to women on issues such as adult learning theories, adult learning models, developmental life stages, women's studies, the woman learner, the executive woman as leader, and the changing role of men and women in organizations. In most of the studies, women are not used as a singular subject of the research, so the models and frameworks that have resulted are not helpful to women in their career progression.

The focus of the research reported in this book is the first of its kind, stimulating interest within and outside the federal government. The demographic data alone provide a basis for a change in the culture of the organization. The demographic trends reflected in the literature suggest that the work force will be of a different composition during the balance of this century and into the next. Women will comprise a major component—61 percent—of this work force. Because of the emphasis on equality in this country, the need to learn more about executive women and their development is more important now than ever.

The research has played a role in making this transition easier. The data document the experiences, learnings, opportunities, assignments, and education that assisted those executive women in the federal government to reach and shatter the government's glass ceiling. Further, it shows what has been important and what has not been important in relationships with those individuals who have influenced their careers while they served as employees, supervisors, managers, and executives./

The research identifies and qualifies the experiences that have helped women executives move into the top ranks in the federal government. The findings reported here identify details about the career progression of these women in government, which elucidate their style of management, their orientation toward people (relationship versus task), and their characteristics of success. This information can guide the development of career growth programs to assist other aspiring women executives of the government. It also increases the visibility of women leaders at the top level of management, who can serve as an inspiration for others.

The public sector can develop its best and brightest leaders to serve the public. Through careful design and planning, programs using the data reported here will groom future government women leaders as well as other women who strive to be in top management ranks. It is essential to understand their patterns of development and growth and what enabled them to shatter the glass ceiling.

NOTES

1. Robert B. Denhardt, *Theories of Public Organization* (Irvine, CA: Brooks/Cole Publishing Company, 1984).

2. P. V. Delker, "Governmental Roles in Lifelong Learning," *Journal of Research and Development in Education* 7 (Summer 1974): 24–33.

3. William B. Johnson, *Workforce 2000: Work and Workers for the 21st Century* (Indianapolis, IN: Hudson Institute, 1987), 95.

4. R. Gross, *The Lifelong Learner* (New York: Simon & Schuster, 1977), 16.

5. David A. Kolb, *Experiential Learning* (Englewood Cliffs, N.J.: Prentice-Hall, 1984), 38.

6. Morgan W. McCall, Jr., Michael M. Lombardo, and Ann M. Morrison, *The Lessons of Experience: How Successful Executives Develop on the Job* (Lexington, MA: Lexington Books, 1988).

7. Kolb, ix.

8. Ibid.

9. Michael M. Harmon, *Action Theory for Public Administration* (New York: Longman, 1981), 52–55.

10. Kolb, 132.

11. Otto Kroeger and Janet M. Thusesen, *Type Talk° or How to Determine Your Personality Type and Change Your Life* (New York: Delacorte Press, 1988), 5–12.

12. Ibid., 52.

13. E. A. Burtt, "The Status of World Hypothesis," *Philosophical Review* 6 (1943): 590–604.

14. Kolb, 117.

15. Malcolm S. Knowles, *The Adult Learner: A Neglected Species*, 3d ed. (Houston, TX: Gulf Publishing Company, 1986), 55–61.

16. Malcolm S. Knowles, *The Modern Practice of Adult Education from Pedagogy to Andragogy* (New York: Cambridge, 1980), 83–87.

17. Chris Argyris, *Reasoning, Learning, and Action* (San Francisco: Jossey-Bass, 1982).

18. Chris Argyris and Donald A. Schon, *Organizational Learning: A Theory of Action Perspective* (Reading, MA: Addison-Wesley, 1978).

19. R. M. Smith and K. K. Havercamp, "Toward a Theory of Learning How to Learn," *Adult Education* 28 (1977): 3–21.

20. Donald Schon, *The Reflective Practitioner* (New York: Basic Books, 1984), 328.

21. R. H. Dave, ed., *Foundations of Lifelong Education* (Elmsford, NY: Pergamon Press, 1976), 35–36.

22. Leonard D. White, *Better Government Personnel: Report of the Commission of Inquiry on Public Service Personnel* (New York: McGraw-Hill, 1935), 3.

23. Floyd W. Reeves and Paul T. David, *The President's Committee on Administrative Management on the Federal Government* (Washington, DC: U.S. Government Printing Office, 1937), 121.

24. Frank D. Ferris, "Is the Senior Executive Service Viable?" *Public Personnel Management* 18 (Fall 1989): 355–373.

25. Chester A. Newland, ed., "Professional Public Executives and Public Administration Agendas," *Professional Public Executives* (Washington, DC: American Society for Public Administration, 1980), 16.

26. U.S. Office of Personnel Management, *The Senior Executive Service*, SES 88–1 (February 1988), ii.

27. U.S. Civil Service Commission, *Biography of an Ideal: A History of the Federal Civil Service* (Washington, DC: U.S. Government Printing Office, 1976), 160.

28. Emily Taft Douglas, *Remember the Ladies* (New York: G. P. Putnam's Sons, 1966), 50–51.

29. U.S. Civil Service Commission, 161.

30. Ibid.

31. Douglas, 87.

32. Homer L. Calkin, *Women in the Department of State: Their Role in American Foreign Affairs*, Department of State Publication 8951 (Washington, DC: U.S. Government Printing Office, 1978), 2.

33. Douglas, 114.

34. Ibid., 77.

35. Ibid., 58.

36. Ibid., 130–144.

37. Calkin, 3.

38. Douglas, 99.

39. Ibid., 120–123.

40. U.S. Civil Service Commission, 161.

41. Ibid., 164.

42. Ibid., 163.

43. Douglas, 144–147.

44. U.S. Civil Service Commission, 162.

45. Douglas, 125–127.

46. U.S. Civil Service Commission, 160.

47. Douglas, 166.

48. Ibid., 102–104.

49. Calkin, 18–19.

50. U.S. Civil Service Commission, 165.

51. Calkin, 24.

52. Douglas, 200–201.

53. Calkin, 24–25.

54. Douglas, 204–205.

55. Calkin, 167–168.

56. Douglas, 196–206.

57. U.S. Civil Service Commission, 168.

58. Jaclyn Fierman, "Why Women Still Don't Hit the Top," *Fortune*, July 30, 1990, 40.

59. U.S. Office of Personnel Management, *The Profile of the Senior Executive Service* (April 1988), C-1.

60. Peter T. Kilborn, "Labor Department Wants to Take on Job Bias in the Executive Suite," *The New York Times*, July 29, 1990, A1.

61. K. Patricia Cross, *Adults as Learners: Increasing Participation and Facilitating Learning* (San Francisco: Jossey-Bass, 1981), 24.

62. Judith C. Hoy, "Learning in the Workplace: A Study of the Settings and Resources for the Learning of Executive Women," Ph.D. diss., Columbia University, 1989.

3

The Research Question

Why have women not moved rapidly up the ladder into top management? The search for answers to this major question leads to the importance of learning about how women who have made it to the top of organizations did so.

The research on women in government, especially at the top management levels, is very limited. Most reports—those conducted by the Office of Personnel Management (OPM), General Accounting Office (GAO), and Merit Systems Protection Board (MSPB)—have examined the programs, the pay, the attitudes, the status, and SES issues. Very little is available on executive development or career progression by the SES cadre. And except for a single study done by the Department of Health and Human Services, none researched top management women. The survey poll done by *Government Executive* in 1988 on the progress of SES women looked at both career (those with tenure) and noncareer (those appointed) women. Some of the demographics from that poll were compared to the data included in the study reported in this book.

Over the past two centuries, many fascinating stories have been told of how women have contributed to society and to government, yet little information is available documenting how the women did it and if there was a pattern to their success. The effort to understand what happened in the past, whether there is a framework for how women learn, and how women make it to the ranks of leadership has been influenced by the work of Thomas Kuhn. His book, *The Structure of Scientific Revolutions*, provides the initial thinking and groundwork for determining the framework of theory to use. Kuhn believes there is a time when science does not explain a phenomenon, and what he calls "extraordinary science" takes over. It is subjective to some, yet Kuhn says that it is based on traditional values that are open to various interpretations by different people; perhaps, he says, "disciplined subjectivity" is as close as one can get to truths at certain times in the exploratory process.[1] It is this thinking, arguing, and persuading that offers and allows the shifting and accepting of a new paradigm to take hold in a culture.

Another scholar instrumental in creating the research techniques was Jay D. White, who proposes a different alternative to the scientific approach.[2] His theory provides a base by which to understand how descriptions and critiques contribute to increasing knowledge. Each of the three models he discusses—positive, interpretive, and critical—is used to explain, interpret, or reflect the findings about the career progression of the executive woman.

THE GOAL OF THE RESEARCH

Based on the descriptions and anecdotal information furnished by 78 SES career women, the purpose of the research was to discover the experiences and learnings that contributed to their career progression. Insights into the public sector as a workplace and how women made it to the top were added discoveries. A comprehensive description of how these women progressed, how they learned, the experiences that contributed to their success, who helped them progress, and how they succeeded in shattering the glass ceiling emerged as patterns.

THE RESEARCH QUESTION

What career pathways (routes, learnings, experiences) were used by women to achieve the status of a career executive in the SES cadre? The research explored which of the experiences made a difference, what lessons were taught by these experiences, where the lessons were learned, and how they were used to shatter the glass ceiling in the federal government.

THE HYPOTHESES

The implications of the research question were explored through many variables associated with career development, human behavior, organizational behavior, public service, executive women, bureaucracy, and similar factors, none of them controlled. The question was whether these variables, in combination with each other, could be studied and provide data appropriate for analysis. This question was considered as the following hypotheses were formulated:

Hypothesis 1. There is a pattern of career progression for SES women that correlates to the research of adult learning theories.

Hypothesis 2. Common patterns of career progression are associated with the successful entry into the SES.

Hypothesis 3. The experiences in the careers of SES women played a role in becoming successful in attaining SES status.

Hypothesis 4. Certain events will make a difference in how SES women have succeeded in government.

Hypothesis 5. The CCL study of private-sector men and women executives can be replicated in the government with SES women.

Hypothesis 6. The private-sector women executives and the public-sector women executives are more similar than different in their experiences.

The hypotheses play a major role in the implications of this research in the federal government and public administration in general.

RESEARCH DESIGN

Although various research designs explored the issues that surrounded the research question and the hypotheses, Jay White's interpretive research on causal relationships was the key in understanding the social relationships and the recognition that through observing and comparing to others, one can learn and take action to increase one's potential. According to White:

> Interpretation seeks to understand the meanings that actors attach to their social situations, to their own actions, and to the actions of others. The logic of interpretation follows the hermeneutic circle in which meaning emerges in recognizing relationships and patterns among wholes and parts. This is a referential process in which something is understood by comparing it to something already known. . . . The basic air of the interpretive model is to develop a more complete understanding of social relationships and to discover human possibilities.[3]

In addition, two social research teams, Guba and Lincoln[4] and Bogdan and Biklen,[5] have demonstrated that qualitative methodology can be used for data collection, especially for surveys or questionnaires and interviews. The strength of a qualitative methodology had been noted earlier in a study by Van de Vall: "The use of qualitative methods in applied social research leads to a higher impact upon industrial policy making than using quantitative methods." Oman and Chitwood further state that "studies that used structured and unstructured interviews appeared to have a higher-than-average level of acceptance."[6] Paul Davidson Reynolds also offers the descriptive strategy as a stage that develops, descriptions of patterns and the survey method as the activity whereby "a collection of people . . . is measured with respect to certain individual characteristics."[7]

The survey research method (questionnaire and interviews) was the means by which information was collected to describe the attitudes, experiences, values, and behaviors of the women in this study. The method depended on their cooperation, candor, trust, and honesty. The questionnaire used was developed for the private sector by the Center for Creative Leadership (CCL), with some minor modifications to reflect more open-ended questions and public-sector language. The questionnaire is descriptive and anecdotal, with 27 major questions covering 5 categories: key events in career, rites of passage, rising from the ashes, the role of other people, and concluding general questions (see Appendix A). This questionnaire served as the basis for a structured interview to gather information on career progression and what had made a difference in rising to the top ranks of government. Of the 78 women who participated in the research, 27 wrote the answers to the questionnaire. This took an average of 2½ to 3 hours to complete. The remaining 51 chose to be interviewed. In the interview, the questions were only clarified when asked; no additional information or explanation was volunteered. The 51 executives who were interviewed were asked three additional questions indirectly addressed by some executives who had filled out the questionnaire:

1. Do you believe there is an invisible barrier within the federal government?
2. Name ten characteristics that you would use to describe yourself.
3. Are there any comments that you have about your career in government that were not covered by this questionnaire?

The other collection source was a cover sheet attached to the questionnaire. It requested generic, demographic information such as name (optional), agency, age, education (major in school and highest degree earned), number of years in the federal government, number of years in the Senior Executive Service, number of years spent at the General Manager (GM) 14 and 15 levels, SES level (1 through 6), and FEI attendance (attendance at the Federal Executive Institute 3-week, 4-week, or 7-week course). The requested demographics were kept to a minimum and focused on the career, not the personal life, of the participant. Instructional information on how to fill out the questionnaire was given. If the participant did not want to write out the answers to the questionnaire, she was given the opportunity to request an interview.

THE POPULATION

The population studied was the senior executive career women in the federal government. This population was selected because of the emphasis being given by *Workforce 2000, Civil Service 2000,* the OPM encouragement of more representation of women and minorities in the SES, and the glass ceiling initiative by the Department of Labor on the private sector. The SES cadre represents the most highly respected and successful people in the federal government; these women would be the critical ones to tell how they became successful and achieved the SES status.

Because of the small number of these women—657 according to the Office of Personnel Management—the questionnaire was sent to the total population.

Many responded that they wanted to complete the questionnaire but lacked time. The following reply is representative:

> Unfortunately, I will not be able to participate in your research project due to the length of time required to complete the survey. Although I am interested in your project and would like to help, I, and perhaps others in your survey, have limited time and would much prefer a survey structured in a way to minimize narrative response.

Of the 657 women who received the questionnaire, 78 participated in the project, enough to replicate the CCL study.

Each senior executive was guaranteed confidentiality of the questionnaire and its data, a crucial consideration for most participants. Many felt the answers to their questions could pinpoint their identity. One executive, who declined to participate, succinctly stated this concern: "Because there are so few women in high level positions, it would be relatively simple for anyone reviewing your research results to figure out about whom you are speaking, especially where the women executives work for a small agency." The complete anonymity granted to each participant was needed to gain her cooperation and enable her to be candid and honest about her experiences within the government. All information, especially quotations, was sanitized to ensure the executive's identity and her career progression were protected. To sanitize the information, all references to any agency, to any employers or congressional committees, to various legislation, and to visible experience or ethical issues were eliminated. In some instances, specific anecdotes were not used in the text to protect identity.

GATHERING THE DATA

These 78 SES women represent 33 different agencies (military, large, and small agencies); 10 field locations and the Washington, D.C., area. Seventy-two women are white, five of color, and one Hispanic. It took five months to do the interviews and to receive the completed questionnaires. Although every interview was taped, very few executives were reluctant to answer the questions. They were comfortable in discussing their careers, their experiences, and their future. As they reviewed some of their experiences, many women found the interview therapeutic. Some became emotional as they dealt with painful memories. However, many seemed energized by reviewing their career successes. The majority expressed satisfaction that they had participated and that the process had been beneficial to them.

THE ANALYTICAL PROCESS

The study began with a review of the CCL studies and their major components—the lessons, experiences, and events of the research—which provided examples of experiences, events, and learnings described by the private-sector women. This information, along with CCL's gender difference data, offered insight on how to be consistent in interpreting the data.[8] The CCL definitions of the events and categories of lessons learned were used to guide the classification of the data submitted by the SES career women, with the definitions expanded as necessary to include specific information directly related to the federal government. For example, the event Starting from Scratch was expanded to include creating a bill, following it through Congress, and being responsible for implementing and/or enforcing the project. Another addition in this category was designing and creating a new division with new programs, such as setting up a laboratory, establishing a center, or setting up a new function. The key event and lesson definitions used to analyze the data provided by the executive women are set out in Appendix B. The bracketed information within the definition in the appendix reflects the information added to the CCL definition. All data provided by the respondents were fit into these 16 key events and 33 lessons (Tables 3.1 and 3.2).

Each incident (key event) cited by the executive and each lesson learned by the incident were registered on a matrix for each respondent. These 78 separate matrices were then combined into a single one showing the total experiences and lessons learned by these women. A total of 305 key events and 1,356 lessons learned were cited, representing 4.4 lessons per event and 17.4 lessons per executive.

The anecdotal data provided by the women were incorporated into the analysis to explain the experiences that made a difference in their careers, the lessons that were learned, and those that they felt mattered in their career progression.

Table 3.1
Key Events

First Supervisory Job
Managing a Larger Scope
Project/Task Force Assignments
Turning an Organization Around
Line to Staff Switches
Starting from Scratch
Career Setbacks
Changing Jobs
Personal Trauma
Employee Performance Problems
Organizational Mistakes
Bosses/Role Models
Values Playing Out
Purely Personal
Coursework
Early Work Experience

Table 3.2
Lessons

All about How Government Works
Balance between Work and Personal Life
Basic Management Values
Being Tough When Necessary
Building and Using Structure and Control Systems
Confronting Employee Performance Problems
Coping with Ambiguous Situations
Coping with Situations beyond Your Control
Dealing with Conflict
Dealing with People over Whom You Have No Authority
Developing Other People
Directing and Motivating Employees
Getting People to Implement Solutions
Handling Political Situations
How to Work with Executives
Innovative Problem-Solving Methods
Knowing What Really Excites You about Work
Management Models
Managing Former Bosses and Peers
Persevering through Adversity
Personal Limits and Blind Spots
Recognizing and Seizing Opportunities
Self-Confidence
Sensitivity to the Human Side of Management
Shouldering Full Responsibility
Strategic Thinking
Strategies of Negotiation
Taking Charge of Your Career
Technical/Professional Skills
Understanding Other People's Perspectives
Use and Abuse of Power
What Executives Are Like
You Can't Manage Everything All Alone

THE STATISTICAL ANALYSIS

For the demographic data, the Statistical Analysis System (SAS) software provided the statistical means, ranges, and frequency distributions for the respondent group. This information presented the profile of the SES career women in this study. SAS was also used to perform a Spearman's rank correlation analysis of the frequency of occurrence of the lessons learned. This analysis determined statistically whether there is a correlation between the public- and private-sector executive experiences.

The software, Lotus 1-2-3, version 2.0, analyzed the data for the qualitative research. The calculations show that the information and knowledge collected by the questionnaire reflect patterns in the respondents' career progress that did not occur by chance. The key events made a difference in how these women were successful in shattering the glass ceiling and becoming an SES member.

SUMMARY

The idea for this research began in October 1989; the women were selected as the population in June 1990; the mailing list was completed in October 1990; and the data collection phases were completed on April 19, 1991. The magnitude of this research and the time to work with the bureaucracy warranted a myriad of techniques to overcome some barriers of gathering the data on a small yet visible population. The use of the CCL data, especially the original research materials, and the CCL gender report, was instrumental in structuring and analyzing the information. Extreme care was made to document as much of the research methodology, the survey process, the data gathering, and the analysis as possible so that others might extend this research and provide more knowledge about how the glass ceiling can be and is broken within major organizations and bureaucracies.

NOTES

1. Thomas S. Kuhn, *The Structure of Scientific Revolutions*, 2d ed. (Chicago: University of Chicago Press, 1970).

2. Jay D. White, "On the Growth of Knowledge in Public Administration," *Public Administration Review* (January-February 1986): 15–24.

3. Ibid., 16.

4. E. G. Guba and Y. S. Lincoln, *Effective Evaluation* (San Francisco: Jossey-Bass, 1982).

5. R. C. Bogdan and S. K. Biklen, *Qualitative Research for Education* (Boston: Allyn and Bacon, 1982).

6. Quoted in Ray C. Oman and Stephen R. Chitwood, "Management Evaluation Studies: Factors Affecting the Acceptance of Recommendations," *Evaluation Review* (June 1984): 302–305.

7. Paul Davidson Reynolds, *A Primer in Theory Construction* (New York: Macmillan, 1971), 155–157.

8. Ellen Van Velsor and Martha W. Hughes, *Gender Differences in the Development of Managers: How Women Managers Learn from Experience* (Greensboro, NC: Center for Creative Leadership, 1990).

4

The Learning Domain

We live in an instant society. We want instant breakfast, lunch, and dinner; instant experiences; instant information; instant news; instant careers; and instant success. Yet this is not reality. Experiences and learning take time, and careers are worked on, at, and through; none happens overnight. Nevertheless, we want to know shortcuts to success and to get on the fast track in our careers. There is a high demand to learn, to know, and to integrate these factors into our daily lives.

The learning of these 78 executive women in the areas of management skills and leadership competencies and how these made a difference in their careers is the theme of this chapter. The learning domain was part of the basic foundation for understanding how the women achieved success and arrived at the top ranks of public service. The lessons these women defined showed their beliefs, behaviors, education, and on-the-job training, as well as which lessons made the difference while they climbed to the executive tower. It showed which lessons are important to learn, how and where to learn the information, and when and where to exhibit these learning skills and leadership competencies.

THE LESSONS OF THE SES CAREER WOMEN

Answering the questions and reflecting on their career progression made the women aware of what they had learned and what types of lessons mattered in their careers. These lessons were those they reported as being essential to navigating their way through the bureaucratic environment to achieve success.

Each woman identified at least three key events in her career that made a difference in the way she managed now. For each event, she described what had happened and what she learned from it (for better or worse). From these answers, 33 lessons were categorized as part of the management portfolio that the woman built throughout her career. (For a complete descriptive definition of each of these lessons, see Appendix B.)

The lessons learned were described in many ways: some made lists, some were very descriptive, some occurred early in their careers, and some took place in their present career position. Examples of some of these lessons follow:

> As a junior manager, on a whim, interviewed for a senior position, for which I had no experience or credentials—was grilled by a team of tough senior grey hair types. Used the only "ammo" I had—wit, insight and assertiveness, and a touch of femininity. They eagerly offered me the job. I turned it down.

> *Lesson:* Style counts more than substance. Assertiveness with finesse pays off.

> As a junior manager, preparing for a presentation on a hot issue to my agency's leadership, went overboard in loading briefing materials with too much detail. My mentor helped me to scrub it down to the key points and focus on "selling" my preferred course of action.

> *Lesson:* Know your audience. Identify the bottom line and focus on it. Leave extraneous information out, however relevant, and handle the flow-through or peripheral issues yourself. Use negotiation and salesmanship techniques if you want to be perceived as a leader rather than a technician.

> Early in my career, finding myself in positions requiring me to (a) give speeches before large audiences, and/or (b) negotiate with hostile, politically powerful outsiders, have learned:

> *Lesson:* Do your homework; know the facts. See the issue from their point of view and prepare to counter. Do not be intimidated by anyone or anything. They would not ask you to speak or come to a meeting if they did not want something. Never lose your cool; stay pleasant, mature, and professional.
> Several stories provided indications of other lessons learned.

> Early in my career, I constructed a major legislative proposal relating to the financing of programs for which I was responsible. It was discussed with and cleared by every relevant federal department and agency and by the White House. It was, however, badly received in the Congress, which felt that it had been taken by surprise and not invited to participate in the preparation. The "official" rules foreclosed that, but no matter. The proposal got no place.

> *Lesson:* What I learned is that one cannot ever discuss with too few—and that official procedural rules need a little bending some times in order to achieve a useful result.

I undertook to persuade the Secretary of my Department to take an action—important in my area of operations—that he didn't very much want to take.

Lesson: I learned, not for the first time, that the key in such situations is (a) to simplify, simplify, simplify the problem; and (b) to relate it to a few principles from which one ought not to deviate. I succeeded in persuading the secretary to "do the right thing."

I was a relatively new Special Assistant to a Deputy Director. We had been asked to assist the Department in a large computer procurement, and I was given the assignment. Although having good technical skills, I had little procurement experience. A group of experts was assembled and reviewed the Request for Proposal (RFP). I felt we could advise the [x], and they could finalize the RFP for solicitation. One of the team members went to my boss and told him the RFP was completely inadequate, and the project was headed for disaster. My boss set me down, got my interpretation of where we were, and then straightened me out. I reformed the team and got them committed (time and emotionally) to the project. After months of hard work and tremendous pressure, a contract was successfully awarded.

Lesson: I had failed to fully grasp the condition of the RFP. I had underestimated the political importance of successfully awarding a contract that fiscal year (the "x's" job was at stake). I had failed to pull together a real team and become its leader.

A new branch was being formed by merging staff from several organizations. The branch combined data and voice communications and was responsible for operations and planning. My boss wanted me to become the chief of the new branch. Although I had led a planning study, I had little hands-on experience with the technology. There was a man who was technically more qualified for the job, but my boss did not have confidence that he could manage the major changes that needed to take place. I took the job, and the branch achieved several major accomplishments over the next two years.

Lesson: I had to make the man who was not selected for the job feel valued. Management skills were more appreciated than technical expertise. I could accomplish outstanding technical accomplishments if I had highly qualified people working for me and if I could motivate them.

Over the years, I observed the positive effect on an organization of having a long-range plan and stated, widely distributed information on where the organization is going and expectations about performance and relationships.

Lesson: I learned that, given a receptive environment, sharing a vision or clear direction can gain support in an organization as well as clarify priorities.

While trying to raise two children, I was selected as a Branch Chief which was my first supervisory position. I was put in the position of creating a program from the ground up. I not only had to hire the staff, but I had to deal with all of the logistical issues—space, telephones, furniture, etc., to set up an office. I also had to market and sell to the external private-sector vendors the importance of the product. It was a horrible job, but it made a bigger contribution to the public's safety.

Lesson: I learned anything is possible. I did not know anything about the technicalities of the product. It is possible to put together a program you are unfamiliar with when you have the right support.

These stories of the lessons the SES women learned were repeated throughout the anecdotes given by the total population. The following 14 lessons were reported most frequently:

All about How Government Works

Self-Confidence

Technical/Professional Skills

Handling Political Situations

Directing and Motivating Employees

Sensitivity to the Human Side of Management

How to Work with Executives

Coping with Ambiguous Situations

Recognizing and Seizing Opportunities

Persevering through Adversity

Developing Other People

Taking Charge of Your Career

Management Models

Coping with Situations beyond Your Control

These 14 lessons accounted for 61 percent of the total lessons reported. The next cut-off—20 lessons cited—represented 78 percent of the total lessons. These are the additional six lessons:

Shouldering Full Responsibility

Getting Other People to Implement Solutions

Strategies of Negotiation

Innovative Problem-Solving Methods

What Executives Are Like
Basic Management Values

These lessons clustered around categories that demonstrate the qualities of executive leadership and connect the lessons.[1] Five cluster groups were established—Setting and Implementing Agendas, Handling Relationships, Basic Values, Executive Temperament, and Personal Awareness—and the lessons were categorized in the clusters as follows (the top 20 lessons are identified by an asterisk and are listed in order of frequency):

Setting and Implementing Agendas
- All about How Government Works
- Technical/Professional Skills
- Shouldering Full Responsibility
- Innovative Problem-Solving Methods
  Strategic Thinking
  Building and Using Structure and Control Systems

Handling Relationships
- Handling Political Situations
- Directing and Motivating Employees
- How to Work with Executives
- Developing Other People
- Management Models
- Getting Other People to Implement Solutions
- Strategic Negotiations
- What Executives Are Like
  Dealing with People over Whom You Have No Authority
  Confronting Employee Performance Problems
  Dealing with Conflict
  Understanding Other People's Perspectives
  Managing Former Bosses and Peers

Basic Values
- Sensitivity to the Human Side of Management
- Basic Management Values
  You Can't Manage Everything All Alone

Executive Temperament
- Self-Confidence
- Coping with Ambiguous Situations

- Persevering through Adversity
- Coping with Situations beyond Your Control
  Being Tough When Necessary
  Use and Abuse of Power

Personal Awareness

- Recognizing and Seizing Opportunities
- Taking Charge of Your Career
  Balance between Work and Personal Life
  Personal Limits and Blind Spots
  Knowing What Really Excites You about Work

The 5 clusters showed the similarity of these lessons and their interconnectivity. The top 20 lessons reported as critical to the women's successful careers represent the major components of executive work. Each lesson was addressed from the perspective of the definition and the relationship within the cluster.

All about How the Government Works

The top-cited lesson by the SES women was All about How the Government Works, the first lesson of the Setting and Implementing Agendas cluster. The definition of this lesson included knowing about the organization: its function, its mission, and its structure and systems. To be successful in government, the SES women believed that it was important to know how the government works, and they began to learn this lesson with their first jobs in government. The federal government has its own methodology of doing business and is accountable to the public. How it operates, functions, and interacts with the public was addressed by many of the respondents. When the executive knew the system, she was able to be more confident in how she performed her planning, budgeting, human resources, and other functions.

> I had an exemplary teacher with the highest standards of performance; she taught me a lot about the ways of government and how to fit in successfully.

> Anybody who is in a position such as mine has to learn that the political and executive micro-management that exists in the Federal Government is phenomenal. You have to anticipate and cover as many of your bases as possible. It's a fact and if you can't adjust, it could eat you alive!

> I worked hard, 12 hour days and 6 days a week; it took a lot of dedication to learn the system. It was a burn-out job.

I possess the historical context of my job. I have worked in a variety of assignments—head of operations and policy; got to create policy and then see it implemented in operations. Utopia in policy is not the same as in operations. Important part of my career has been understanding the system. I believe this is why it has been so smooth sailing for me.

No matter how high you go in government, you must understand the process and the system. It is important to know the details and specifics of what you can manage. Much of my success has had a lot to do with knowing the details of the system.

I walked into a job and an environment that was foreign to me. I wanted to live there, so I had to learn their mores, culture, and system. I made an analogy that I was living in a foreign country to help me work with the system. It served me well.

I have built a reputation for learning rules, the system, and how it works so I can be effective without peril (or a minimum of walking on thin ice).

I did leadership research for years and modeled myself accordingly. I picked and chose key points and added them to my data bank. I picked up institutional wisdom and became a savvy practitioner.

Understanding the system of government and how it operates was a prominent lesson among the executive women; this knowledge built their reputation as an expert, gave them visibility, and contributed to their self-confidence. This lesson was considered the foundation by which the executive began her climb up the ladder. Figure 4.1 shows the events (Managing a Larger Scope, Scope; Starting from Scratch, Scratch; Project/Task Force; Bosses; and Changing Jobs—for complete definitions of all of the terms in the figures in Chapters 4 and 5, see Appendix B) where this lesson was learned. It also makes a comparative analysis with private-sector women executives and how they learned as compared to the federal women. The event Managing a Larger Scope was cited by the private-sector women as making a difference in helping them learn about their organization. The remaining events did not impact the private-sector women in this instance.

Self-Confidence

Getting or having Self-Confidence was the second-ranked lesson. Defining self-confidence led to a litany of reflections that gave the women a feeling of respect, integrity, self-esteem, and accomplishment. Many of these lessons overlapped with one another, and the self-confidence lesson almost emerged as a completion of learning a particular lesson. For example, learning about the system of government and being proficient enough in it to work the system gave the executive self-confidence in herself and her abilities. Having a good founda-

Figure 4.1
All about How Government Works

Events

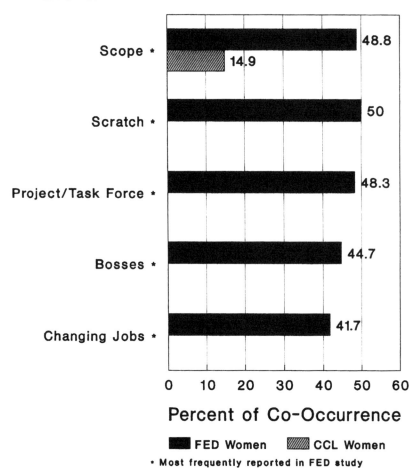

Source: 1991 Survey of FED Women Executives by D. M. Little

tion about what the agency was about provided the executive with the knowledge that she was part of the organization and her role was important in meeting the mission of the agency. Self-confidence was required to project credibility. In a Keri Product Group–sponsored survey of 6,000 men and women, which covered 5 major areas of confidence—confidence building how to's, appearance and image, relationships, workplace, and crises—Judith Briles reported in *The Confidence Factor* a strong correlation between working status and a woman's feeling of confidence. Confidence can be learned, and it can be gained through maturity and experience.[2]

These 78 SES career women had self-confidence, developed as they matured through experiences and increased their knowledge professionally and personally. These women substantiated the findings of *The Keri Report*: "Among all the factors in a woman's life . . . life experiences (and its crises) were identified as the most critical in the development of confidence."[3] Confidence did not seem to be inborn but was developed by and through events that occurred in the lives of people. The more the executive displayed her confidence, the more successful she seemed. This heightened confidence bred more confidence to try new things, take risks, and take command of new and risky situations. The lesson of self-confidence was clear from anecdotes:

To implement a Federal program you must have inner resources. I realized my answers were just as viable as others. I emerged with a sense of confidence and made it happen and did it just as well as others.

I can do anything I want if I can define it.

Receiving larger assignments and promotions helped increase my confidence.

I readily accepted an assignment to positions about which I knew very little, learned about them, and performed in a manner which made me a logical choice for promotion to a more responsible position. I have done this several times in my career, e.g., I made a change from the function in which I was very knowledgeable, to a function about which I knew very little. This change was made at the Assistant Division Chief, top management, level of the organization. From making moves of this kind I have gained confidence in myself that I can conquer new areas of responsibility, perform well, and have an impact. This experience has made me accept subsequent assignments with little hesitancy. Success reinforces.

I trust my instincts—if it doesn't feel right, I don't do it. It goes with self-confidence. I take risks and expose myself to new ideals.

I always felt I could deal with things.

I was able to pull off a major special event. It was a major happening in the scope of things for that area and the town. To end up being the focal point for all the planning for this event and carry it off with all the significant Republican politicians in the state, plus the town, and emerge as the real organizer of the event made me realize I had the potential and skills to move into bigger areas of management.

In my early years I had difficulty saying "no" and shied away from difficult situations. I have grown into someone who can say "no"—who can take a difficult situation and address it head-on in a tactful, diplomatic way. I now look at what wide-range impact my actions may have.

My job was to pick things apart which sometimes meant having confrontations. This was required to give them [the political appointees] what they wanted. I worked well with them because I respected who they were; I was comfortable with myself and how I approached the problem to get the information.

I get nervous when I speak before large audiences so I took a public-speaking class. It helped me to do a better job and also gave me confidence.

This lesson of self-confidence, the first lesson in Executive Temperament cluster, carried through to the other lessons. Self-confidence made the person feel successful in attaining the goal that was pursued. These women worked on building their confidence. They learned what they needed to accomplish a certain task, knew where their weaknesses were, and designed how they could acquire the knowledge that would make them successful. To many, part of being an executive was projecting an image of confidence and knowing that they could do the job. Figure 4.2 shows the sources by which the executive women learned and how they compared to the CCL study of the private-sector women executives.

Technical/Professional Skills

Lesson 3, Technical/Professional Skills, was part of the Setting and Implementing Agendas cluster. The foundation of this lesson was competency in one's field of endeavor: law, medicine, research, personnel, finance, management, administration, health, engineering, computers, accounting, labor relations, human resources, or something else. This lesson was defined accordingly: learning a technical or specialty content area, being recognized as an expert, or keeping up with new technology.

It was a technical challenge due to the scope of responsibility (all voice and data communications) and the criticality of making operations work.

I learned all about the budget business—GS-7 to GS-11—writing the program, preparing justification, worrying about the budget cuts, and executing the budget. I always worried about the budget being cut, but I never had one cut drastically.

Came into government as a GS-7, took FSEE [Federal Service Entrance Examination], moved into a personnel staffing specialist position, and acquired expertise in all areas of personnel.

Figure 4.2
Self-Confidence

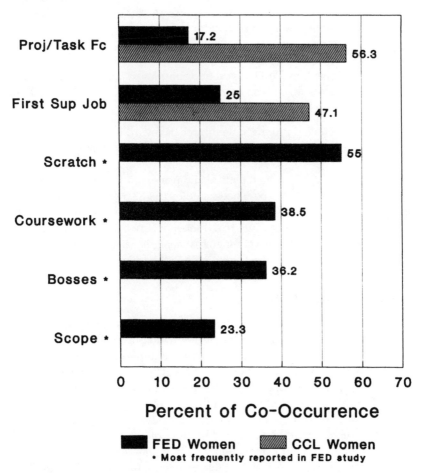

Events

Source: 1991 Survey of FED Women Executives by D. M. Little

[Has a doctorate in electrical engineering] I went from a novice to an expert; I was known as an international expert in the field and invited to different countries regarding the "black box."

The law profession helped me analyze problems faster and taught me to be theoretical and to look at all aspects of the problem.

In the acquisition business you tread a fine line providing customers new services and maintaining checks and balances.

I had to manage a hi-tech area with a lot of contracting—both areas in which I had not been involved before. I didn't even understand the terms and acronyms which were being used. For the first two months I had to do mental simultaneous translation for the acronyms.

I acquired a technical credential.

When I received my Ph.D. it gave me confidence, and now I could take my place as a scientist. In an agency of scientists and engineers, one must have a Ph.D. to have credentials.

I wrote a technical report on computer password techniques—was the basis for master's thesis and for subsequent Federal standard.

These examples of acquiring technical and professional skills to do the job are repeated throughout the experiences cited by the SES women. Their technical and professional expertise paved the way for them to move up to, and sometimes into, different careers. Figure 4.3 shows where this lesson was learned by these women. It also shows a comparative analysis with private-sector women executives and how they learned compared to the federal women.

Handling Political Situations

Another important lesson—the highest-rated lesson in the Handling Relationships cluster—was Handling Political Situations. In government this lesson stood out as the women described the political implications of their positions, their careers, and their successes and failures. This lesson encompassed the full scope of politics, from working with a political appointee through to and including confronting the political agenda of the administration and using the political system to carry out the function of the organization. Many women executives noted their careers had been capped because of a political appointee; others were at one time in their careers political appointees and could appreciate the political process. Through some of their anecdotes, the complex world of political power and its importance emerges:

The political appointee needed me to translate the technical skills for him and to give history behind the issues.

I was asked to work for a political appointee. I soon realized he wanted me to be his hatchet lady. I told him I would not do this. I was hanging out without a protector. He wanted me out of the way so he could bring someone else in to do the job.

I failed to clear it "politically."

Figure 4.3
Technical/Professional Skills

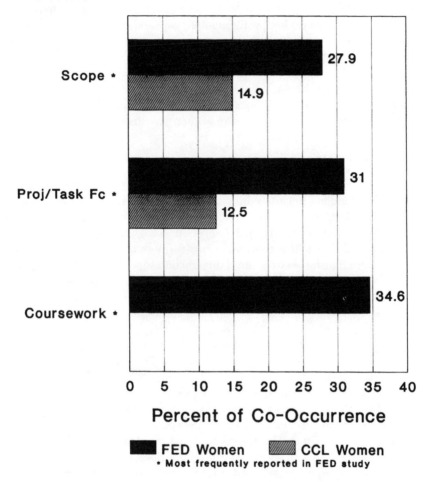

Events

Scope * 27.9 / 14.9

Proj/Task Fc * 31 / 12.5

Coursework * 34.6

0   5   10   15   20   25   30   35   40

Percent of Co-Occurrence

■ FED Women   ▨ CCL Women
• Most frequently reported in FED study

Source: 1991 Survey of FED Women Executives by D. M. Little

I learned the political system and not to be an idealist.

I learned to be more savvy to "p" issues. I learned to be more savvy in working the system and not to be confrontational.

This administration is difficult to work with. They want to cut out career people. The political appointees want to go to all the meetings. They don't know as much, but this is what they want.

The knowledge of how to work within the political system and to understand the political ramifications of a job played a significant role in how the women progressed up the ladder in government. Many who stood up to political appointees or went around the chain of command found their careers set back. One SES woman was fired during a change in the administration; another was transferred and instructed to keep a low profile; another kept a low profile because she was affiliated with the "wrong party" (the party not in power). Women who knew how government worked and knew how to play the political system were considered on the team. One woman who was selected by a political appointee knew that without his support she would not have been promoted into the SES. Figure 4.4 shows the sources by which the executive women learned and how they compared to the CCL's study of the private-sector women executives.

Directing and Motivating Employees

The next-ranking lesson, Directing and Motivating Employees, also falls within the Handling Relationships cluster. In this lesson, the women discussed how they staffed, managed, and directed their staffs in order to build a team and organization. They also addressed delegation, recognition, competence building, responsibility, and accomplishments through others. Many of the SES women were transferred to or hired directly into supervisory and management positions where the staff was demoralized, there was a reorganization, the unit had problems, or there was a new mission. The following story depicts some of the challenges that came with directing and motivating a staff:

> I was moved by management into an existing branch with a mandate to make some changes in mission and approach. The previous manager was well-liked by the staff and was a good friend of the most competent employee in the group. I proceeded to try to build the required capability but was being undercut to some extent by my staff. This finally resulted in a "showdown" or very frank discussion between me and my key employee (who possessed some skills I needed). What resulted was a mutual agreement that: (1) I am the boss and will set priorities; (2) staff has important contributions to make and needs to have opportunities for more involvement in decision-making; and (3) since we both care about both the people and the mission, we have to figure out a way to work together. When I am insensitive to "people" issues, he needs to let me know so we can deal with the problem. In my next job, the first thing I did was have one-on-one meetings with staff to get their input on problems, changes, and priorities. I also made a special effort to listen to senior staff within the organization and not make unnecessary changes without input and discussion.

The executives directed and motivated their staffs in a variety of ways:

Figure 4.4
Handling Political Situations

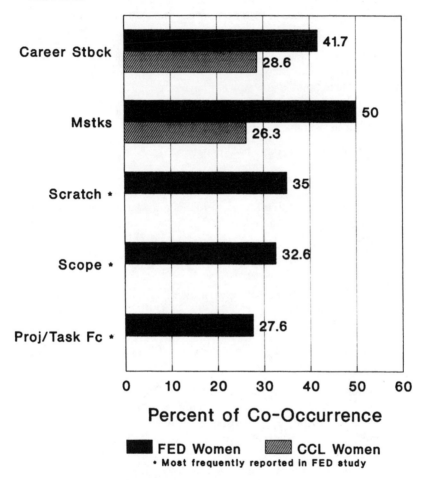

Events

Source: 1991 Survey of FED Women Executives by D. M. Little

I love dealing with people—seeing people grow and learn, getting things done as an organization and as a team.

I see myself as an expeditor. I realize other people are better than I am who are on my staff, and I am comfortable letting [other] people take over.

I feel confident and comfortable to rely on others. I set up a plan and get people to help me.

I tried to take on the role of a laissez-faire manager. Found out in managing professionals that you must give them opportunities to allow creativity and have balance and to foster teamwork and to try to not be an oppressive manager, but play more of a facilitating role.

It is common sense to me to direct others to do things. Total Quality Management is common sense, an opportunity to work with people, to direct them and lead them, a new way to manage agency and empower others.

Making people work as a team. Pushing people to physical limit. Do the job and be answerable for it.

Delegate responsibility and hold people accountable. Don't do it all yourself.

Moving from managing a small group of people who were doing work that I had done or was trained to do to managing a large number of people doing work I was not trained to do. This move forced me to learn how to delegate, how to ask the right questions, and to think about how to make sure that between my subordinates and me there was a complementing skills match.

Get people to buy in, help develop a recommendation, and issue a draft for comments to defuse any hostility. By doing this, I learned how to manage a multi-faceted organization.

Need to deal with group dynamics, climate of the group, and be a teacher and facilitator.

Important to give of yourself to your group. Need to build them up and get better results from people. Complimenting people more than calling people on the carpet. People respond better to praise than criticism. You accomplish goals better that way.

The directing and motivating employees lesson was important in forming relationships that could get the job done. Some women believed that the interpersonal skills required to form a team were vital to accomplishing the mission of the organization.

Sensitivity to the Human Side of Management

The lesson Sensitivity to the Human Side of Management fell within the Basic Values cluster but also formed a bond with the Handling Relationships cluster. This lesson showed how the women displayed warmth and caring about their employees and an understanding that their staff have needs and lives outside work. Many of the women related how they tried to be fair with staff and put themselves in their employees' shoes. The women felt it was important to learn about their employees and to take their unique skills and qualities into account when forming teams and projects.

> People need stroking. Became more sensitized. To make best use of staff, I must be sensitive to people.

> I try to see the other side of the story.

> I learned that many times people yell when they are insecure, that the best way to solve a problem is usually to discuss it, that people respect you when you are capable and honestly trying to support them, that when you are open with someone they are likely to be open with you, and that by taking responsibility for a problem you are more likely to get help solving it than if you blame it on someone else.

> I am sensitive to other people's feelings. I have found that by reading body language and seeing people's behavior that managers and supervisors can react and learn about people. I have high expectations and give people feedback.

> I don't believe you should treat people well by making their job easier. Put more things on them so people can show what they can do.

> [Based upon her past experiences] if she became a manager she would make sure she would keep up with the process and provide people with feedback and make changes early on in the policy process so people wouldn't be surprised.

> As a senior specialist, I took the job seriously and shaped others' careers and trained them correctly. I tried to give them a good start and showed them I was interested and cared for them.

> Never do for people what they can do for themselves.

> [I] like situations where I am open with others and share information; this office operates with or without me. I want people in the pipeline to take over. Take a step back and see what quality of people I have. Now there are 6 or 7 people who can step in and do my job.

> Everyone is an individual, and you must figure out the strategy to get things accomplished.

Many of the women who had children discussed how this experience helped them be more sensitive to their employees.

> Having children makes me more sympathetic to people.

Having two children as I worked helped me develop a sensitivity of needs of people in the work place, and then I would try to accommodate those needs.

I learned a lot—juggling demands of home and work.

Children help balance me and slow me down. I can identify with people who have families and be more understanding.

Having a baby has made me more approachable. I focus on making time and keeping things even.

I have a division of 35 people; my experience as a mother is great, because I now have 35 kids; the more I work here the more it is true.

Very seldom have unproductive time.

When these women were faced with the need to cut staff or budget, conduct a reduction in force, merge organizations and cut out the deadwood, or perform the wishes of a new administration, they found they had to draw on all of the lessons they had learned about sensitivity to deal with the affected employees and their families and also staff who remained after the cutbacks. To some, this process was the darkest hour of their careers. Learning this lesson and working in a negative environment imprinted on many that there has got to be a better way to run the government. Many came up with more humanistic alternatives the next time they had to make cutbacks and through these differences helped to maintain a more productive work force.

How to Work with Executives

How to Work with Executives ranked next in the Handling Relationships cluster and links the previous two lessons. Knowing how to work with executives in a positive manner helped pave the road for a smoother ride up the career ladder. The women learned this lesson through many contexts: giving presentations and briefings, knowing when to push and when not to push, focusing on the skills to persuade, and leading the boss to move in their direction. Some of the women were very adept in this lesson; they had started early in their careers. This lesson was instrumental in the SES woman's being perceived as credible and competent. Although they may have been competent and experts in their specialty, if they did not have this lesson, they could not articulate their views. Also, their knowledge was rarely counted in the decision-making process. If the woman did not use her deportment skills, she was not regarded as effective and competent.

The first time I went before the Director of the Office of Management and Budget with budget overviews, I persuaded him to my point of view. I also knew when to argue with the Attorney General in order to come to a resolution.

Had DOD [Department of Defense] give me a "dog and pony" briefing so I could understand what things meant. After the briefings I would still ask tough questions on what were you doing or how were you doing x, y, z.

[Every time] a new agency head comes in, I learn that person's requirements and try to meet them.

Don't leave yourself open. To get there, couch things in a way of sharing and saying, "these are our options, and this will get you there." To the extent things are reasonable, you are flexible.

Learned how organization worked; important to present things a certain way. Know what key managers are effective. Get insight of the culture of the organization.

In '70s you couldn't use the softer approach, the command style was in vogue; but in the '80s, I had to be less directive to get things accomplished.

I wrote a humorous report to the Director. I thought I might get repercussions of it, but, instead, the top executive said if I could effectively use humor, then I could probably write other things. I started getting different assignments.

Value of being well-prepared to defend something.

Learn to play to next level up, but don't undermine the person in the middle. Let people know what is being done regarding the project.

Ability to know when to keep mouth shut.

It is a stressful experience to interact with high-level executives. I learned how to strategize and get points across without wasting their time.

Aware of the importance of how I am perceived. Concerned about my image and understand it doesn't matter what I say, but it is what I do that makes a difference.

Know how to manage him, improve coordination, and then carry it out; know who to support and then speak up at meetings.

Never say "no"; say "let me see what I can do about this and reasons we can't do it."

Within this lesson, the women were exposed to high-level executives early in their careers. They learned how best to approach them, what the requirements were of the position, and who had the power. From these experiences, the women built their portfolio to include how executives work.

Coping with Ambiguous Situations

Another Executive Temperament lesson was Coping with Ambiguous Situations, which had two sublessons: (1) putting out fires with inadequate knowledge is possible in a turbulent context and (2) learning new skills is possible while integrating the old skills, even in new and uncertain environments. To learn either one or both of these, flexibility and knowledge on how to operate in an uncertain environment were required. Many of these learnings in this lesson came from maintaining an efficient organization during political changeovers, reorganizations, and job changes. Some of the lessons emerged from the value system and culture of the organization.

> I went to a broken office. I grew more as an attorney there than during any other two years of my practicing. First, I saw an entirely different approach to many problems, which showed me that either there were many ways to achieve various goals or reinforced the importance of doing them the correct way, in those situations where the new way was incorrect (made me understand why the way I had learned to do them was right). Second, I was quickly promoted to oversee the work of numerous, extremely inexperienced attorneys and to try various cases. This was at the same time that my immediate boss was fired and never replaced. So I was receiving very little support from above. I was over my head but had to deal with it and did. The whole experience really forced me to do only what was important, which, of course, required me to figure out what was really important.

> There was a value system within the organization that I didn't understand. The organization gave mixed messages. They said, "do what I say, not what I do." I learned to be flexible; I learned the organizational culture and how to work the organization and get things done. I learned a lot those first years.

> Changed jobs and found self in deeper than what I thought. I never ran an accounting operation before. Shortly the deputy left; I tailored the position and became a strong financial manager.

> Colleagues call me an ad-flex person [a person who goes out of his or her way to be flexible and responsive]. Known for finding ways to be responsive.

> I had to do a major regression analysis research project without the knowledge of how to do it. I was over my head. I learned to rely on others to get the information and to find out the answers.

I survived the changing of administrators seven times. I learned to be flexible and hold true to my personal ethics.

Being able to cope with uncertainty and remain flexible was a critical lesson, especially as the top of the career ladder became nearer. Some women said their flexibility and self-confidence helped them take chances in trying new projects or taking on a new job even if they were not technically qualified for it. They learned to take advantage of situations and seize opportunities.

Recognizing and Seizing Opportunities

Recognizing and Seizing Opportunities, the first lesson in the Personal Awareness cluster, was important and made a difference in the career path of these women.

I received an opportunity through a combination of luck, perseverance, and ability—probably in that order. I first learned that [my agency] had a slot at the National War College (NWC) through a casual conversation. National security was an area of interest to me. I learned that the agency's slot for the coming year had not been filled and asked my supervisor to nominate me. Although an outstanding employee, I clearly lacked the background in national security programs possessed by most NWC nominees. However, partially because I was a woman and the director was under some pressure on EEO [equal employment opportunity] issues, and partially because I had some support from other senior managers, I was selected to attend. Not only was this experience beneficial in terms of broadening my personal knowledge and experience base, but it was also an important "ticket" to be punched in my career progression. I returned to the agency and was much better prepared to contribute than I would have been prior to the War College experience. I learned that one often has to make her own opportunities; and, if you really want something, you have to keep following up on it, or it won't happen.

Taking full advantage of an excellent mentor early in my career (he was several levels senior to me in the agency), got "entry" to the behind-the-scenes interchanges among senior officials—learned that decisions and deliberations on extremely complex and sensitive issues were often done with little, but essential information, in a very informal (occasionally "flip") environment—and that the key factors influencing decisions were less policy or budget, and more politics and personal positioning.

Look for the right opportunities and take them.

I had the right opportunities; I got to work on some interesting things that allowed me to work across the board. Opportunities to be exposed and to work on different applications.

The awareness of an opportunity required the executives to know their own strengths and weakness and to know how to capitalize on them. Some of the women said they were at the right place at the right time, but if they had not known what they were capable of doing, they would not have been able to recognize and seize the opportunities that made a difference in their career progression. In some cases, the women were aware they were given special opportunities (because of their gender or because of who they knew) but did not feel comfortable in taking the opportunity at that time. They felt they needed more experience, more education, or just more time. They considered themselves lucky when other opportunities were available. Others felt they should have taken the opportunity no matter how they felt about being prepared and worked hard to learn what was required to get the job accomplished.

Persevering through Adversity

The next ranking lesson was Persevering through Adversity in the Executive Temperament cluster, which incorporated finding ways to accomplish goals in the face of barriers and obstacles. It also required the women to recognize that adversity can be overcome through hard work, dedication, and commitment to the job or project. Risks were sometimes incurred, and sometimes the women worked long hours to see the task accomplished by the deadline. Many accomplished great feats with few resources, little support, and inadequate staff. Some felt strongly that their very survival was in jeopardy.

> I launched a major international study in the face of jealous opposition of division colleagues. Resulted in a decided success for the [agency] and for me professionally—caused a great deal of personal stress at work and at home for at least a 5- to 7-year period.

> Aggressively pursued an initiative that my agency's leadership strongly wanted, in the face of much opposition and hostility from the affected private-sector industries—while knowing there was a weak link in our position. Did not insist aggressively enough that we confront and do whatever was necessary to seal the gap; found ourselves confronting litigation targeted right on the weakness.

> I entered an atmosphere I knew nothing about. I was left with a mess in my lap and had to adjust to it. You can imagine the microscope I was under. I learned I cannot shadow box with rumors. People will embellish and most will fabricate. Don't be defensive or encounter every rumor. You know you have integrity and make decisions to keep on a steady path. Can't answer rumor mill. You will be reacting to rumors instead of being proactive. I kept the long-range goals in mind and made a go of the situation.

More than 10 percent of the respondents noted that others were "out to get me," that they were on the "political out," and they were concerned about surviving in the public sector. At the same time, they were aware of the implications of their project for the public welfare and were committed to doing the job right. Many of the women felt it was an ethical decision to stand up for what they believed, and they were willing to take the consequences. Some of them did this at personal risk and had a career setback. But as difficult as the crisis was, each believed she was a stronger person and more knowledgeable because of the political "whitewater" experience.

Developing Other People

The next lesson, Developing Other People, included providing employees with training and helping them grow. This facet of their job gave the SES women opportunities to learn and offered them the environment to make changes and develop their skills. This category, and the other lessons in the Handling Relationships cluster, showed the importance of developing people and suggested how to do it.

I consider it essential to establish early on the strengths and weaknesses of subordinates, so that I can develop them in areas where it is needed and so that I can accurately assess what my level of confidence should be.

I bring people up through the system. I tell them you must be better than good; and, when you are, you are armored to fight the system. You must be willing to make the system work for you and have it be responsive to your own goals. Look at the system in very practical ways. Systems are there; keep in mind they aren't aimed at you. I learned you can change the system and try to emphasize to my people in developing them that one person can change the system—you just need to know the system and the needs of your organization.

Almost a legacy—you pick them, select them, teach them to do it right and send to training programs—more chances to produce competent people.

Walk around and know your people. Must go around and be seen. Talk to the people.

I was elated about one of my branch chiefs getting an opportunity to be acting regional director but at the same time hated to see her leave. One thing I learned was not to hold people back.

More people skills are required to deal with staff in place. I worked with them and was able to develop the people's management skills.

I am a big believer in employee development. I practice it and put resources to it—a long-term investment in people.

The women executives reported this was one of the areas where they have the most fun as managers: watching their subordinates grow, providing them with opportunities to explore a varied mixture of assignments, and exposing them to different levels of people.

> Enjoy seeing staff progressing in their careers and evolving. Help them explore what they like and point them in direction to advance to what they want to do. Everyone should tailor their career on their personality and their talents.

> [I have the most fun] seeing my staff grow, develop and progress.

> I love to hire, develop, and promote—and pull out potential leaders. I am delighted when people do well. I love watching people grow.

> Seeing people grow. When I have confidence in staff, I will throw them in front for the experience.

> Matching the right person to the right job—Great!

> Helping people develop and taking people to different stages.

Taking Charge of Your Career

The next lesson, Taking Charge of Your Career, was part of the Personal Awareness cluster. Its main components were to know when to take charge of the situation and to take charge of one's career. At one time or another, each executive addressed experiences when she knew it was time to take charge and move out of her job. Sometimes the job was too comfortable, sometimes it had become stale and routine, and sometimes a new experience was needed. In all of the cases, the woman moved and found something new or different. Following is one executive's technique for taking charge of her career:

> You visualize how you would like things to be years down the path, and you spend time daydreaming your vision and make it a part of everything you do. Enhance everything you do by incorporating the vision. If I do this, it will get me closer or further away to what I want to do. It worked!

Another executive examined her career and learned some lessons that she could use later:

> For the first eight years of my government employment, I was on a temporary appointment in which continued reappointment was determined annually. Retention was determined by performance and utility to the unit where I was assigned. I had no job security, no title, and an uncertain future—I took nothing for granted. Lessons learned: (1) Put more energy in

the job that needs to be done than in creating dependency on the people who have temporary authority over your professional career. They fade away, but your long-run performance remains. (2) Try to do the right thing as you understand it. Speak truthfully and without undue concern about whether you are telling someone what they want to hear. (3) Avoid wasting time dwelling on people who have failed to support you or have opposed you—forget past problems, and look to the future. (4) Be fair when it comes time to supervise and manage.

Executives who wanted to be part of an organization or to play a particular role searched out opportunities:

> I realized that here was an avenue—being part of these planning efforts would expose me to all levels of the organization. It opened my eyes to what was going on in the organization. Here are some contributions I can make. Asked to participate on the project. Became a member of the director's team.

> I went on a detail to a policy area. I felt uncomfortable. I feel more comfortable with long-term development projects. I had to accept and know who I was and what I could do. I knew that I was not a policy or staff person, but a line person.

In giving advice, the women encouraged others to identify where they wanted to go to realize their career goals. One executive cautioned not to stay in any job too long; instead, find jobs that will provide exposure and get pegged as a doer. An executive called each experience an "opportunity to grow; and, if you don't jump in the water and learn to swim, each time you will miss out on something of value."

Management Models

The Management Models lesson was another chain in the Handling Relationships cluster. Through learning about the major management models and theories, the executives learned different perspectives on how to manage. One executive expressed her theory regarding management:

> To me, the learning of management is the most underrated program going. Technical efficiency is easy. Understanding what is necessary at the right time and diagnosing what is needed is the art. It gave me a different dimension—a lifetime profession. Values change; organizations change (growth)(reduction). Be always learning.

Other executives voiced alternative ways they learned management models and the effect on their careers:

I thought I knew everything, but I learned a lot about new management models. The training made me more secure in what I did and what I knew.

I had to develop as a manager. Learned about matrix organizations, how to manage programs, the impact on organization, and how we make people feel part of it and accept it.

Learning that the behavioral ground rules and the factors influencing decisions are completely different—the transition from super-technician to executive manager.

My continuing education (history, science, art), with the constant example and assistance of my husband, has helped me to see the common underlying dynamics in all things, and to keep day-to-day circumstances on the job in their proper larger philosophical context. Certainly improved my insights and instincts, and my sense of humor!

Knowing management models and applying them on the job provided the executive with self-confidence in doing her job and helped her feel more competent in her role as a manager.

Coping with Situations beyond Your Control

Coping with Situations beyond Your Control was a hard lesson to learn. Most of the women thought they could cope with most situations, until they recognized that in some of them control was not possible, and nothing they could do would change the system or the situation. Operating within unrealistic expectations and dealing with uncontrollable environments and frequent "changing of the guard" made the executives realize that some things are not controllable. This recognition was a big step and helped them overcome some of the frustrations. The ways they chose to operate in this kind of environment varied: avoiding the situation, getting involved in new projects, redefining the situation, or leaving the job. In some of these situations, the women expressed the role of luck, fate, and timing in being at the right place at the right time or the wrong place at the wrong time. The executives' temperaments sometimes made the difference in how well they coped with the situation. They learned, for example, that they could not be confrontational or too visible, and they could not take on challenges out of their field of expertise. They also learned what they could do: know themselves well enough to realize how they reacted in these kinds of situations and to be aware of how they were being perceived and then take action to deal with the circumstances.

Can't seem to get control of the situation. The goals keep changing. I drop back and punt, but that is not dealing with it effectively.

You walk a delicate line.

When situations are out of control, I feel frustrated. I walk through division and sit in someone's office and chat and ask them, "What's up." Spending time with my people is energizing and helps me cope.

Feeling powerless as programs which have consumed my professional life were transferred to another federal agency.

Tried to get people to work together but couldn't. Had a "Pollyanna" attitude that people can be turned around.

Writing policy (regulations, guidelines, answering questions) in a highly complex area. It became "special" when the underlying laws suddenly changed in a major program reform, and I was the only one who knew enough to figure out the transition and assess the impacts. I became "famous" overnight. (Luck helps.)

Realize that some things are worth fighting for and some are not.

One executive described the lesson of coping with situations beyond your control from a different perspective.

I was transferred from a top-level job to another job. I learned who my friends were (the ones who kept in touch) and how important it is to support other executives, male and female, who run afoul of whatever situations might be out of their control.

In coping with these uncontrollable situations, the women felt stronger and more competent, especially if they recognized the situation for what it was and did not get so frustrated that it interfered with their own sense of well-being.

Shouldering Full Responsibility

Usually the women who believed they coped well with situations beyond their control had also learned the lesson of Shouldering Full Responsibility. They implemented their program agendas, stood up and took issue, and knew their limits. They took risks for their group and assumed full responsibility for the situation.

I had responsibility for all the work. I needed to figure out how to face up to the situation and stay and correct it.

I was responsible for a new organization. Oh my God, you realize that you are responsible for doing it all; and no one knew how to do it; and so you were able to exercise what you want to do.

Knowing that major administrative changes were needed and no easy way of doing, I decided to implement, knowing I would take a lot of "flack."

The wrong button was pushed, and the wrong version of a controversial issue was given out to the press. I volunteered to resign. I learned to personally check every small detail before it is released. I feel very vulnerable to small things.

I did all of the oral arguments in the Appellate courts and represented the United States—it was all on my shoulders.

Getting Other People to Implement Solutions

Although the women learned to shoulder the responsibility and get the task done, they still interacted with their staffs to get them to implement solutions. The next lesson, Getting Other People to Implement Solutions, involved a shift in focus from individual task performance to managing others in order to accomplish a task. The recognition that others can make or break a manager and that they can make the difference in accomplishing the mission's function was the major lesson learned: people are important and should be treated accordingly. Some of the women learned this lesson as they realized that for the first time in their career they needed other people. They could not be the analyst or the technician but needed to be the manager and work through their staff to accomplish the goals.

As GM-14, given independent responsibility to set up an entirely new function—with only money, 35 "slots" to hire people, and a vague idea of mission. Congress wanted it mobilized in 6 months, and my boss was in the hospital. I did everything from the gruff administrative details to defining the broader policy implications. Rather than trying to do it all "hands on" myself, I learned to find, train, and use good people to do it for me. (I learned to manage, through baptism by fire.)

When I came to this job, I tried to manage like the boss I replaced. I tried to boss people around like he did, but I felt very uncomfortable. So, I decided to manage; like I would manage and if they didn't like it, that was too bad. I also can, and know when to, be sweet and charming instead of commanding to get things done.

Don't try to be the best analyst when you are the manager. If you are good, you can do what you are asking others to do. Don't have time to do other's jobs. When employees find you are competing with them, they will not do their best. Keep this perspective if you want others to get the product out. Staff is under pressure; it is your job to relieve this pressure. Do things that will help them get the job done.

There was so much pressure, I had to depend on others to get the job done.

I felt confident and comfortable to rely on others. I set up a plan and got people to help me.

This lesson fell within the Handling Relationships cluster and showed the importance of knowing the value of others and the role they play in a manager's success in an organization.

The people who make me look good are my staff, and I need to continue to give them the support they need. I am a conduit for them.

Good performers can be left alone. They are self-motivated and are off doing their own work. With pressure-intensive jobs, supervisors and managers can do harm by yelling at people, by not having patience, and by not supporting them.

I am no longer a technical expert—in a way that makes me feel insecure. I can't keep on top of technical ins and outs and must depend on staff.

Strategies of Negotiation

Another lesson in the Handling Relationships cluster was Strategies of Negotiation, whereby the women learned how to deal with various external groups: Congress; unions; the public, local and state government; interest groups; lobbyists; the White House; OPM; Office of Management and Budget (OMB); other government departments; the press; academia; industry; scientific communities; private businesses; and private entrepreneurs, within the United States and internationally. These women learned how to use different tactics to negotiate with these groups and made themselves aware of different approaches for different people as well as different circumstances. Formal negotiations were considered a skill that could be learned. These negotiations could be adversarial and collaborative, depending on the client, the customer relationship, and the stakes involved. Most women discussed their experiences with winning favor (or not) with Congress and negotiating the budget with OMB. The awareness of the best tactics required to "play the game" was instrumental in the outcome of the negotiations.

Called upon to champion/defend/promote technical programs to Congressional staff, OMB, and Department of Commerce.

Disappointed with some of the compromises made with OMB. Felt like we were selling [my agency] down the road.

Deal with a lot of outside consultants. In charge of transactions. Wanted to get answers, but business demands would outweigh the going through with the deal.

Involved in all contract negotiations.

Use negotiation and salesmanship techniques if you want to be perceived as a leader rather than a technician.

Came to blows with company representative. Issue came to an end. I believe [I should have] been more sensitive to the situation.

Negotiation skills are important [in dealing with the public]—sometimes need to be reasonable and compromise.

Strategies of negotiation overlapped into many of the other areas of the executive's work. Learning what strategy to use with each group was important to the outcome. One executive gave an example of the importance of knowing the group when the chief negotiator refused to argue and negotiate with women. She told him: "If you don't negotiate with me, we don't negotiate." Most of the women did not describe such explicit examples but provided information about how they asked questions, debated the issues, checked the best approach, and proceeded to steer their course to make the most of the negotiation, whether with unions, Congress, private industry, or the public. The goal usually was to obtain "something"—resources, people, money, policy changes, a new bill, a new plan of action. How effective the executive was perceived in this endeavor and how she handled herself during the process sometimes afforded her the credibility and visibility needed to pull her out of the group and to be given choice assignments.

Innovative Problem-Solving Methods

This type of visibility and credibility was gained through another lesson, Innovative Problem-Solving Methods, which was about doing things differently, taking risks, finding new approaches, and thinking out of the ordinary channels and coming up with a solution to the problem.

Organizations still highly regard fire fighters. Can look like a hero if you can clean up a problem. Problem solvers are still valued.

I walked into branch; everything was wrong. Thought of ideas to straighten it out. I was able to implement these ideas (held a lottery).

Having a large organization to manage and to get to experiment. Hopefully people don't know you are experimenting. I can see how different styles impact on organization and see some of the strengths and weaknesses. I can see what works.

It is clear that innovative problem-solving methods fall within the Setting and Implementing Agendas cluster. The executive women who solved major problems in their organizations usually took risks and were willing to shoulder the responsibility if the idea did not work. Performing the mission within the organization—getting the job done and meeting the deadline—was their focus, but many described how creative approaches to solving the problem led to successful projects. Very few discussed failures in using an innovative approach, but some admitted that maybe they blocked failures out of their memory. For many, doing something new and creative changed their approach to management. They used these methods again as they moved up the ladder.

What Executives Are Like

The next lesson, What Executives Are Like, provided the woman with insights into the working life of an executive. They saw the positive and negative sides of executives' lives, their values, their likes and dislikes, their mode of operation, their behaviors, and their vulnerability. In most instances, the women had been around high-level executives throughout their careers. Many had thought it very natural and "no big thing" working with the top (they took it for granted), and many were involved in activities that regularly had high-level executives in attendance.

Almost in awe of political appointees, congressional people and those in the Hill world; but, when into it, it is rather boring.

As I got to know more and more executives and spent time with those in the "evening gown competition" I was disillusioned by their scope of thinking and how bureaucratic they were.

At first, the head of the agency was impressive to me. Now I work with them all the time and am not intimidated by them.

Involved in Reform 88—it gave me insight into skills and lack of skills of what characterizes high-level executives; also gave me good insight into political aspects.

One executive gave this advice to younger managers on how to manage their careers by knowing what executives are like.

Learn "what's different" about technicians versus executives—the differences in what's important to them, how they interact—learn the importance of personal style, psychology, salesmanship, camaraderie, and self-confidence without hitting others below the belt.

Basic Management Values

The last lesson that made up the 78 percent of the lessons learned by the 78 career women was Basic Management Values. It provided the ideal values, practices and undesirable practices, or management values or principles that guide appropriate, ethical behavior as a manager. Examples of this lesson indicated integrity, trust, and credibility that a manager must exemplify.

> I learned to make decisions based on what is good for the agency—or ethically and morally correct—not based on whether or not someone will "like" you. Also consider what would happen if everyone did it—and if I do this what is the worst that can happen, and can I live with it.

> Values are ingredients to be successful and do not go out of fashion. I am not trendy—What is right is right and I don't switch. Do the right thing.

> I thought my role in government was to tell them. Now, more of a facilitator and really have to stop and give them support and realize must step in and say you can't do it. I don't write CYA [Cover Your Ass] memos.

> I grew up with a set of ethics. You did the best you could and had respect for people; had honesty and integrity, and, by doing that, people knew my standards. I am easy to work with. Worked hard enough so I wouldn't be afraid to accept my paycheck.

> Differences in values—not understanding values of professionals versus those in the manufacturing business.

> I was touched by the turmoil going on in the political arena during Watergate. I realized how fragile positions are. Top one day and the next day at the bottom of the heap. Knew a lot of people who were hurt in this scandal. Things stopped in government.

The issue of ethics in the government played a prominent role in the careers of these SES career women. Some made a stand for their beliefs and their value system; some refused to take the action; some worried so much that they quit the project and asked for a transfer; and some were forced out of their position.

> I feel I have integrity. I said if you do this, I will resign.

Other Lessons

There were 13 other lessons learned, each representing less than 2.5 percent of the total number of responses by these 78 SES women. They follow in rank order:

1. You Can't Manage Everything All Alone was the discovery that managerial jobs cannot be done alone.
2. Dealing with People over Whom You Have No Authority stated that sometimes you must be able to get cooperation from others over whom you have no control.

3. Strategic Thinking was seeing a broader picture of the organizational scope, usually in a longer time frame. It can contribute to national well-being.

4. Confronting Employee Performance Problems was a lesson that many of the executives addressed when they discussed procrastinating, because they learned they should move quickly in confronting people about their performance.

5. Dealing with Conflict was part of the manager's territory. Conflict can be dealt with in three ways: avoiding it, resolving it, or reducing it. The awareness of the origin of the conflict helped deal with the situation.

6. Building and Using Structure and Control Systems was the realization that structures and systems can be designed to run without them, and they did not have to manage every phase of the day-to-day operations.

7. Balance between Work and Personal Life encompassed the realization there is more to life than work and learning the importance of relaxing and discovering by examining and reflecting upon past work life and what gives meaning to one's life.

8. Being Tough When Necessary was taking a stand even if it meant firing someone. It held people accountable for their work.

9. Understanding Other People's Perspectives dealt with people other than in the immediate work group and required understanding their perspectives, recognizing that individuals are different in culture, in language, and in skills, being sensitive to these types of issues, and acting accordingly.

10. Personal Limits and Blind Spots was coming to terms with personal limitations, such as time, resources, or lack of expertise.

11. Knowing What Really Excites You about Work was learning all about yourself and what you like to do enough to discover what is exciting and worth doing on its own merit.

12. Use and Abuse of Power was recognizing that the use of power can help or hinder the attainment of the goal.

13. Managing Former Bosses and Peers occurred when the executive was promoted over her peers and bosses and how she operated in this different and sometimes stressful role.

EXECUTIVE IMPORTANCE

The definitions and some of the anecdotes given by the SES career women, the 33 lessons, and the 5 clusters they fell under revealed lessons that make up careers. A closer inspection of the clusters reveals that there were top lessons learned by these women in each category: Setting and Implementing Agendas (4 of the 6 lessons), Handling Relationships (8 of the 13), Basic Values (2 of the 3), Executive Temperament (4 of the 6), and Personal Awareness (2 of the 5). From this information, SES career women learned lessons that helped them perform their organization's mission and run the government in an efficient manner. They were knowledgeable in many areas of Handling Relationships. They realized the importance of people in organizations. They were very value oriented and possessed the major traits of an executive. As they acquired these lessons, their Personal Awareness category suffered. In fact, many thought they may have sacrificed too much for their career.

Each of these 33 lessons was learned by the SES career executive and made a difference in how she shattered the glass ceiling. Some learned these lessons early in their careers, some later in their careers; some through observing others, some by hands-on experience, some by reading, and some by taking courses. The next chapter addresses each of the sources from which these lessons were learned.

NOTES

1. Esther H. Lindsey, Virginia Homes, and Morgan W. McCall, Jr., *Key Events in Executives' Lives*, Technical Report No. 32 (Greensboro, NC: Center for Creative Leadership, 1987), 225–307.

2. Judith Briles, *The Confidence Factor: How Self-Esteem Can Change Your Life* (New York: MasterMedia, 1990).

3. Ibid., 5–8.

5

The Experiences

The lessons the SES women learned were significant to their careers. When these lessons are combined with the source in which the lesson was learned, they make a powerful developmental tool. When the woman knows what she needs to learn (the lesson), she is able to use this knowledge as a development tool to plot how she can get the experience, and who she needs to assist her in achieving her objective. This knowledge can increase the base from which the woman operates. The lessons and events can be her planning guide to ensure she gets the lessons required to make her next career goal achievable. The study identified 16 sources that taught the women executives the lessons that helped them climb the ladder to SES. The first column of the following list of events shows the percentage of lessons learned by the event. The second column indicates the number of women who reported the event as being significant in their career progression. The events were considered significant when a cumulative percentage of 75 percent was achieved. The list that follows shows those sources, in rank order; an asterisk denotes those considered significant:

Events	Percentage of Lessons Learned	Number of Women Reporting This Lesson as Significant
• Managing a Larger Scope	19.1	43.0
• Bosses/Role Models	14.6	47.0
• Project/Task Force Assignments	11.0	29.0
• Changing Jobs	8.6	24.0
• First Supervisory Job	8.1	28.0
• Starting from Scratch	7.4	20.0

- Early Work Experience   5.5   19.0
- Coursework   5.2   26.0
  Turning an Organization Around   4.7   13.0
  Career Setback   3.8   12.0
  Line-to-Staff Switches   2.5   9.0
  Employee Performance Problems   2.3   9.0
  Values Played Out   2.3   9.0
  Organizational Mistakes   2.1   6.0
  Purely Personal   1.5   6.0
  Personal Trauma   1.2   5.0

Just like the lessons, the events (sources of experiences) were clustered into categories:

Assignments
- Managing a Larger Scope
- Project/Task Force Assignments
- First Supervisory Job
- Starting from Scratch
  Turning an Organization Around
  Line-to-Staff Switches

Hardships
- Changing Jobs
  Career Setback
  Employee Performance Problems
  Organizational Mistakes
  Personal Trauma

Other People
- Bosses/Role Models
  Values Played Out

Other Events
- Early Work Experience
- Coursework
  Purely Personal

Each of these sources was distinctive enough to stand alone; in combination with the others, they composed a larger picture of the activities occurring in the careers of the SES women. Each category had at least one significant source.

The clusters that stand out were Assignments, in which the women learned a majority of their lessons, and Other Events, which included early work experience and coursework. The SES women had a variety of early work experiences, especially those who had started their careers in government and continued to build and broaden their experience base. In addition, the high level of education possessed by the women indicated that coursework played a prominent role in their career advancement.

A detailed description of each of the development sources follows the narrative. Definitions of the sources were derived from the experiences reported by the executives and from the core definition used in the CCL study (Appendix B). In addition, the top three lessons learned from the source were discussed. (In some cases more lessons were addressed because of ties.)

ASSIGNMENTS CLUSTER

Because of the Assignments cluster's importance in controlling most of the women's work life, we examined the six assignments that made a difference in their careers first. They represented the largest number of sources of experiences discussed by the 78 SES women. They are: Managing a Larger Scope, Project/Task Force Assignments, First Supervisory Job, Starting from Scratch, Turning an Organization Around, and Line-to-Staff Switches.

Managing a Larger Scope

N events = 43 (14 percent of all events)

N lessons = 259 (19.1 percent of all lessons)

N managers = 43 (55.1 percent of all managers)

Managing a Larger Scope, cited by 55.1 percent of the respondents, was a major factor in their career progression. In this event, the manager had a broader and different kind of responsibility than she had ever held before. In fact, many of them reported that the larger scope was their movement into the SES position. Others discussed staff-to-line switches, technical-to-manager switches, and scientist-to-manager switches. All represented changes that included an increase in numbers of people, dollars, or functions managed. Some included a geographic relocation. Most of the managers in some way were unprepared to assume the enormous responsibility and requirements of some parts of the new position. In many cases, the person was a deputy, and within a short time frame, her boss had left, and she moved into the vacant position without adequate training or complete knowledge of the scope of the job. In addition to learning the job on the run, she directed and managed others. While going through this experience, many did not know if they would survive the pressure exerted by the job, subordinates, political appointees, or external pressures of Congress. Nevertheless, these experiences provided them with visibility, credibility, and bonuses.

> I leaped from a non-supervisory role (via a 2-year sojourn covering for my supervisor who was on detail within the agency) to managing a 30- to 35-member staff and a $12–15 million program.

> I accepted a deputy position. After a month, the director left. I didn't know anything. I was asked to take charge of this $39 million program and 800 people. I realized I was responsible for all of this, and I had never managed before. I didn't even have a management style.

> Moving from managing a small group of people who were doing work that I had done or was trained to do to managing a large number of people doing work I was not trained to do. This move forced me to learn how to delegate, how to ask the right questions, and to think about how to make sure that between my subordinates and me there was a complementing skills match.

The top two lessons learned by women in Managing a Larger Scope were learning All about How Government Works and Directing and Motivating Employees. To be involved in these types of leadership roles required the executive to understand the fundamental operations of the government, to understand the system well enough to know what it could do and its limits, and to learn to be flexible. Without learning these lessons, the executive women said they would not have been able to survive some of their Managing a Larger Scope experiences. The importance of knowing how the executive worked within the system was demonstrated by how she directed and motivated her staff. The executive realized she needed to move the organization and the work, and to do this she depended on her staff to do the job. How she directed and motivated her staff to grow and how she created an atmosphere of teamwork became instrumental to how successfully she managed the organization.

> I learned I could survive in such a turmoil. I learned all about the organization, its problems and its people. I coped with the situations by understanding that the people here are my best asset and they can help me—I don't need to be the expert of the system.

> I went from a technical position to SES as a manager. I was here six months, and my boss was pulled to a detail, and I was in charge of an operation. I was in a sink-or-swim position. I tried to maintain the integrity of the system in a positive way.

Four lessons tied for third place: Shouldering Full Responsibility (Setting and Implementing Agendas), Handling Political Situations (Handling Relationships), Sensitivity to the Human Side of Management (Basic Values), and Coping with Ambiguous Situations (Executive Temperament). In each of these lessons, the woman learned how to integrate her style, her past experiences, and her skills to manage a larger-scope job. Each contributed a valuable insight in how to set up the operation, handle the political implications (people and process) of the job, work in an uncertain and sometimes volatile situation, and maintain her sense of common values and sensitivity to others. All of these large tasks were learned while under a vast amount of pressure to produce a product that influenced and sometimes controlled the public's welfare.

Of the 33 lessons, 31 of them were learned in Managing a Larger Scope. Of these 31, 17 composed the cumulative percentage of 79.5 percent for this event. The two lessons not learned were Managing Former Bosses and Peers and What Executives Are Like, which fell under the Handling Relationships cluster. Because of the enormity of the meaning of taking on larger scopes of management, these two lessons were probably learned much earlier than the others in the career progression of the executive (Figure 5.1).

Project/Task Force Assignments

N events = 29 (9.5 percent of all events)

N lessons = 149 (11 percent of all lessons)

N managers = 29 (37.2 percent of all managers)

The Project/Task Force Assignments event was cited by 37.2 percent of the respondents as a key developmental experience. This event incorporated all assignments of short duration that were accomplished alone or as part of a team effort. Many of the assignments had short time frames, ranging from 2 weeks to 2 years, with most taking place over a 3- to 12-month period. Some had fixed deadlines. Those most discussed were projects visible to their superiors, government wide in scope, or having wide ramifications. Many of the individuals detailed to work on these task forces continued to work in their regular jobs as well. This was the first time many of the executives had been exposed to high-level executives. Others said the project provided them with information on what they liked or did not like, and they used this knowledge to take charge of their careers. Some felt that these assignments gave them a different perspective on working with other government executives and others that it provided an opportunity to "strut their stuff."

> I got involved in doing project work for the senior staff people. I didn't apply for positions; I was solicited to do this. Based upon my work, they took an active interest in getting me to take on more responsibility.

> I have been on a lot of task forces—special assistant jobs, special commissions, panels, and project start-ups. I knew I had to do quality work and ensure that I got the credit for it.

Figure 5.1
Managing a Larger Scope

Lessons

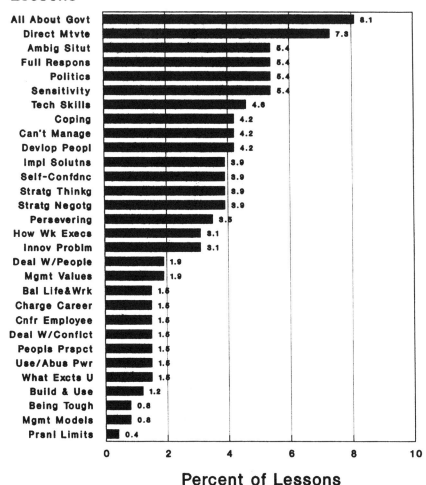

Percent of Lessons

Source: 1991 Survey of FED Women Executives by D. M. Little

There was a crisis situation whereby teams and special task forces could not come up with the answer. My boss felt I could bring a different perspective. My staff and I dug in and tried to understand the problems. We were able to come up with a detailed solution and make recommendations regarding the fix. It was exactly what was needed. My reputation was greatly enhanced by this exposure.

[I was selected to be on an] agency-wide task force. We had six months to pull it off—had to do a strategic plan, had to get a bill passed, had foreign countries surveyed. Received lots of psychic rewards.

Selection to projects and task forces played an important role in the progression of careers and also to learning about the breadth and scope of the federal government. The top three lessons learned from this key event were All about How Government Works (Setting and Implementing Agendas), Coping with Ambiguous Situations (Executive Temperament), and Strategies of Negotiation (Handling Relationships). This event gave the executives the hands-on experience required to make these lessons part of their management foundation. Project/Task Force Assignments helped them learn about their organization, gave them an opportunity to meet others outside the organization, exposed them to different perspectives of a problem from a variety of angles, and allowed them to work on-site at various organizations. The most-mentioned diverse details were with OMB, OPM, the General Accounting Office, Congress, the American Society for Public Administration, the National Association for Public Administration, and interagency task forces.

I was in the right place at the right time to serve on a high-level team. The six months I was on the team was an eye-opener. I had accessibility to high-level executives, and I learned how the procurement system works.

I headed a team of GM-15's inside and outside of my agency to work on an organization-wide program. I was also the lowest graded person. I lacked some of the knowledge required to be the team leader.

For this event, there were 16 lessons taught, for a cumulative percentage of 81.5 percent (Figure 5.2). All but 4 of the 33 lessons were mentioned by the executives when they discussed their experiences on projects and task forces. The four lessons not learned, because of the nature and definition of task forces and special projects, were Building and Using Structure and Control Systems (Setting and Implementing Agendas), Confronting Employee Performance Problems, Managing Former Bosses and Peers (Handling Relationships), and Use and Abuse of Power (Executive Temperament).

First Supervisory Job

N events = 28 (9.1 percent of all events)

N lessons = 110 (8.1 percent of all lessons)

N managers = 28 (35.8 percent of all managers)

Figure 5.2
Project/Task Force Assignments

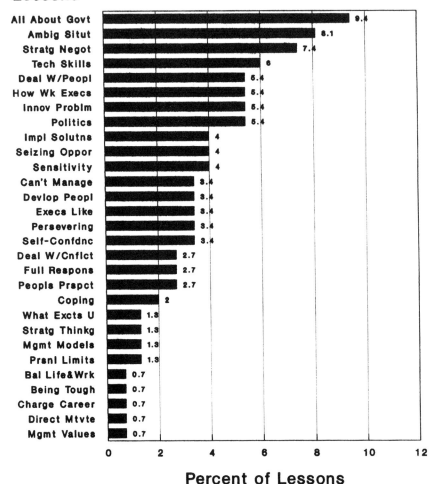

Lessons

All About Govt	9.4
Ambig Situt	8.1
Stratg Negot	7.4
Tech Skills	6
Deal W/Peopl	5.4
How Wk Execs	5.4
Innov Problm	5.4
Politics	5.4
Impl Solutns	4
Seizing Oppor	4
Sensitivity	4
Can't Manage	3.4
Devlop Peopl	3.4
Execs Like	3.4
Persevering	3.4
Self-Confdnc	3.4
Deal W/Cnflct	2.7
Full Respons	2.7
Peopls Prspct	2.7
Coping	2
What Excts U	1.3
Stratg Thinkg	1.3
Mgmt Models	1.3
Prsnl Limits	1.3
Bal Life&Wrk	0.7
Being Tough	0.7
Charge Career	0.7
Direct Mtvte	0.7
Mgmt Values	0.7

Percent of Lessons

Source: 1991 Survey of FED Women Executives by D. M. Little

Within this event, the executives discovered another part of management work: managing people. It was the first time they had supervised anyone and worked through someone to accomplish the mission of the organization. For some, this experience occurred very early in their career, but for others (the majority), this exercise did not occur until they were a GM-14 or GM-15, and for some others not until they had entered the SES ranks. The lessons they learned during this experience mostly dealt with people: Directing and Motivating Employees (Handling Relationships), Developing Other People (Handling Relationships), Sensitivity to the Human Side of Management (Basic Values), Self-Confidence (Executive Temperament), Managing Former Bosses and Peers (Handling Relationships), and Confronting Employee Performance Problems (Handling Relationships). Four of the six lessons fell within the cluster of Handling Relationships, which involved an active role by the supervisor to manage people. The realization that managing was different from individual technical responsibility for a project came as a surprise to some. To others the breadth of supervision and its role in the organization was very important. Although these six represented the top lessons learned, a total of 15 lessons, composing 78.9 percent of all of the lessons learned, were taught by the event of the First Supervisory Job.

> I guess at every stage of my working life I had to take responsibility for something I had never done before; but coming in small chunks and as a logical follow-on to what I had done before; I never felt all alone. When I got my first supervisory job (GS 14), I had to supervise an employee who was older than I, male, and a long-term incumbent of his position and an unsuccessful applicant for mine while I was new to the agency. I knew I had the support of my boss. I knew budgeting. I was open; I was fair; I asked for support, recognized good work, and expressed appreciation for it. I did not expect miracles and realized that it would take time for our relationship to work out. In the end, we had an excellent working relationship.

> Supervised three males who were older than I was, all Ph.D.s. A challenge because they were peers. Learned the importance of respecting people's pride and creativity and being there. Be the person to take away any barriers.

> First supervisory job—a small office of eight women. I didn't like it at first. Learned to hire folks that shored up my weaknesses.

> I learned to manage people, which required tact and diplomacy. Patience was hard to learn. I demanded high standards of self and subordinates.

> My co-workers became my subordinates, and they were old enough to be my parents. I was the new kid on the block, and all of a sudden I was in charge. I operated as a team. Peers need to know you know what you are doing; and, no matter what, you support your subordinates.

> Learned from the people I supervised. People are unique, what works well with one may not work for others. Learn to be flexible.

The First Supervisory Job event was a major stepping-stone in the career progression of the women. It was the first time they had encountered working through others—sometimes over others who were their friends, sometimes confronting difficulties in getting the job done because of lack of money and staff, and sometimes in situations beyond their control. It was a time for them to determine how they wanted to be managed and how they would treat others. For some, this aspect of the job meant giving up their technical or specialty profession, and this was hard to do. Many had someone else, usually a boss, to provide help and advice. Others took courses on supervision and interpersonal relationships to address some of the fundamental management issues that go along with supervisory jobs. In each scenario discussed by the women, the first supervisory job carried more responsibility and gave them more visibility in the organization, especially in how they managed people to accomplish the organizational goals.

Only 3 of the 33 lessons were not reported as being learned within the First Supervisory Job event: Personal Limits and Blind Spots, Knowing What Really Excites You about Work (Personal Awareness), and Strategies of Negotiations (Handling Relationships).

Starting from Scratch

N events = 20 (6.5 percent of all events)

N lessons = 100 (7.4 percent of all lessons)

N managers = 20 (25.6 percent of all managers)

The Starting from Scratch event meant that the executive had a from-the-ground-up project in which she created, built, managed, and implemented a start-up operation. Most of these start-ups were a result of the organization's expanding; some were from new initiatives and programs from Capitol Hill; some were field locations; and some were a new idea that took root. Among the projects were opening a new field office; creating a new department or division; designing and introducing a bill, including watching it pass and implementing it; setting up a new laboratory; establishing a training center; enforcing a new policy; and setting up new functions based on reorganizations. In some of the start-ups the executives were not equipped to do the job and lacked experience, especially on such a large scale.

> [A new piece of legislation was just signed establishing a new program.] I was new to Federal service and given the assignment of developing a viable nationwide program from scratch. It required developing a program, interfacing with high-level managers, and managing resources. Since no one knew more than I did, I couldn't make mistakes, because no one else would know. It gave me an atmosphere for taking chances.

> As a GS-14, I was tasked to set up a [new office] starting from scratch. This was an opportunity and a challenge. It was a clean slate to establish

an organizational structure that made sense. I did broad recruiting and hiring for three-fourths of the jobs.

I installed a new system in an organization. The new system was very visible, had to work the first time, affected most parts of a fairly large organization, and I had only a very general knowledge of the subject matter.

I was able to set up, build, and run my own laboratory.

I established a new center. I laid out the organizational structure, the procedures, and the policy. It had to be started by a certain date and must be finished by a certain date.

I had to open and run a field office.

A creative situation—institutionalizing a brand-new program.

I had to establish a disaster field office—from locating space to staffing and making it operational in nine days and staying on site for six weeks to train staff.

The top four lessons learned in 35 percent of the events described were Self-Confidence (Executive Temperament), All about How Government Works (Setting and Implementing Agendas), Handling Political Situations (Handling Relationships), and Building and Using Control Systems (Setting and Implementing Agendas).

I had the opportunity and the ability to take a new, an unknown area, and be a visionary and put a road map together to carry it out. I figured out how to gather players and orchestrate the details of the plan, then did the implementation of the solutions through others.

The [agency] was given authority overnight to set up rules where there had been no precedence. I was part of the high fliers that were brought together to create an organization and a mechanism to carry out the mission. It was a chance for me to demonstrate how quick and capable I was.

Took a downgrade in order to totally design and build a new program. Had a budget, built-up staff, and decided how to operate. It gave me independence plus program and resource-management experience.

Helped craft and draft a [social welfare] law. I worked on the regulations, created the bill, and was able to also implement it by starting a new branch.

Taking a piece of legislation and building a program around it. Responsible for the entire process—marketing and selling program, procurement system, procedures, hiring professionals, and the technical policy of the program. I learned anything is possible.

There were 27 lessons of leadership learned through Starting from Scratch. The executive took control of the uncertainty of the situation, and using her leadership skills, was able to create, build, manage, and be successful in a major organizational initiative. Sixteen lessons made up 82 percent of the total lessons learned. Six lessons were not covered in this event: Taking Charge of Your Career (Personal Awareness), Confronting Employee Performance Problems (Handling Relationships), Coping with Situations Beyond Your Control (Executive Temperament), Dealing with Conflict (Handling Relationships), Managing Former Bosses and Peers (Handling Relationships), and Management Models (Handling Relationships).

Turning an Organization Around

N events = 13 (4.3 percent of all events)

N lessons = 64 (4.7 percent of all lessons)

N managers = 13 (16.7 percent of all managers)

In this key event, Turning an Organization Around, the executives discussed how they had been selected to restructure or straighten out the problems. The typical situation involved low morale, disillusioned staff, too much work, not enough resources, poor management, incompetent staff, low credibility, integrity issues, no space, logistics, impending reorganization, or abolishment of unit. When the new manager walked into the organization, she realized the enormity of some of the problems. Some were not salvageable, and many of the women reported that this may have been one of the near failures within their careers. In this situation, she had to know how to think on her feet, be willing to take action against the individuals causing some problems, and know when to use toughness as well as a light touch to change the organization. Sometimes the behavior required was not in concert with the executive's way of managing, especially if the style was aimed at consensus building rather than playing tough and making drastic decisions, such as firing the person.

Another Turning an Organization Around event was doing the job without the support of her boss and going around this person to gain ground in changing the structure. Sometimes this was at high risk for the woman, and she may have saved the organization at the expense of her career progression. In these instances, the women related that they had to use all of their persuasiveness in working within these relationships. The important behavior not to display was confrontation and getting involved in adversarial combat. The most discussed Turning an Organization Around events covered the aftermath of a reorganization, a new program initiative using existing staff, new legislation, turnover of administration, or change in political parties.

[I was promoted into this job.] I had to make a lot of hard personnel decisions. There was low morale, and the organization was dysfunctional. I had to set standards and hold the people accountable; people left. They didn't like me very much. I brought the [organization] back to life.

Moved by management into an existing branch with a mandate to make some changes in mission and approach. The previous manager was well-liked by the staff and was a good friend of the most competent employee in the group. I proceeded to try to build the required capabilities, but was being undercut to some extent by my staff.

Rebuilt a division that was under-funded with people and priorities; I was asked to be the deputy. Built a high level of morale. It soon became an area of high visibility sparked by foreign interests. Much of this interest I had caused to happen.

Moved to another program that was in trouble. I had reputation to be someone who could be put in a problem situation and help fix the problem. It was fun to work on these problems.

I was asked to come fix a problem. The [office] was in shambles; I had to do an overhaul of the system while supervising 20 people.

The branch chief was removed, and I was asked to take over a complete disaster branch. Found file cabinets full of checks not mailed. Staff was lousy, and I had to get the branch back on its feet.

Walked into job with a 2- to 3-year backlog. Had to turn person around and let go of manual operations.

Detailed to head an office in another agency. The head had been removed, and the office was in shambles.

Coping with Ambiguous Situations was the top-ranked lesson learned in the Turning an Organization Around event. The executives learned that with only general knowledge and sometimes lack of a particular technical knowledge, they had the ability to turn an organization around. The next four ranking lessons learned were All about Government (learned more about how the system operates), You Can't Manage Everything All Alone (learned how to build up the staff by directing and managing them), Technical and Professional Skills (learned the importance of having a specialty area and understanding the technical intricacies of a project), and Self-Confidence (learned from the success of the turnaround to have more confidence in abilities).

Awkward situation to be in—deputy to person who was removed and took over office that was totally in disarray. Questioned how to get through [this] and clean up this mess. I had to supervise 62 people involving different skills. I had no help from above—depended upon the staff. Experience taught me I was a survivor.

Had to reorganize the office; had to learn about communicating with field offices. I had to get people (political appointees as well as career executives) to buy-in. By lobbying and using my [specialty] experience I was able to turn the organization's function around from a dotted line to direct authority.

Within these turnaround assignments, the executives learned 24 lessons that helped them clean up the messes, act with authority, and deal with a broad range of problems, people, and issues. There were 17 lessons that comprised 88.9 percent of the total lessons learned. Nine lessons were not reported; of these, four fell within the Personal Awareness cluster (Recognizing and Seizing Opportunities, Taking Charge of Your Career, Balance between Work and Personal Life, and Knowing What Really Excites You about Work), four were in Handling Relationships (Management Models, What Executives Are Like, Dealing with People over Whom You Have No Authority, and Managing Former Bosses and Peers), and one was in the Executive Temperament cluster (Use and Abuse of Power).

Line-to-Staff Switches

N events = 9 (3 percent of all events)

N lessons = 34 (2.5 percent of all lessons)

N managers = 9 (11.5 percent of all managers)

The Line-to-Staff Switches event involved moving into a staff position to learn more about the strategies, operations, and culture of an organization. The executives within this event played several significant roles: chief adviser, special assistant, expert in a particular area, policy writer, and ombudsman. The executives who were in these positions were highly visible and had to be "available with the right answer at the requested moment." The breadth of the areas deemed as staff positions ran the gamut of all specialty areas within an organization: law, medicine, research, planning, budgeting, personnel, procurement, space, contracts, quality, science, engineering, health, safety, employment, ethics, regulations, legislation, and others. Sometimes the executive stayed a short time in these areas, but many of the women who had this experience were in the position more than a year; some positions were permanent. Except for some early work performance or the SES position they held now, many women occupied staff positions at some time in their careers. Although these jobs were to teach the executive about strategies and operations from an organizational perspective, many of the women were selected for these positions because of their technical expertise and their capabilities in a certain field.

I was the lone expert in the Office of the Secretary.

Had several special assistant jobs. What you do is work through a principal. You can influence how policy decisions are made. Realize ultimately it is not your decision. Working for [x] I had less independent authority but more influence.

Invited to come and work on a staff as an [x]. I worked on the big-picture issues of the agency and not on the nuts and bolts.

Special assistant to the director involved more interdisciplinary work beyond the social sciences. Instructed senior management where subject matter was not familiar and difficult to comprehend.

Was part of the secretary's staff. In charge of day-to-day office operations. I had historical insights into the organization. I learned to be quick on my feet and how to answer tough questions. I made sure I was fully prepared to discuss all the responsibilities of all offices within the department.

Five lessons (with a cumulative percentage of 50 percent) stood out in this event. Two tied for first place: Handling Political Situations and How to Work with Executives, both in the Handling Relationships cluster.

At the GS-14 level, I was pinpointed as the main contact person in the [department] for a nationwide initiative. Dealt with high-level executives and had a lot of responsibility.

Moved from deputy director of a small division to role of a staff advisor to "high profile" executives.

Moved from an operational to a policy environment. Responsibilities now global, responsible for policy department-wide. I had to learn the politics of the organization and the environment. I was visible to the top layers. Operated under unrealistic time frames with limited resources. Pressures go into personal life. You have to become an organizational person.

I was selected to be a special assistant; the political appointee needed me to translate the technical aspects for him and to give history of the organization.

The other three major lessons were tied for second place: Technical and Professional Skills (Setting and Implementing Agendas), Persevering through Adversity (Executive Temperament), and Taking Charge of Your Career (Personal Awareness).

I became director of a program staff office and had to work closely with line office directors. I learned patience and the importance of "selling" ideas for program and organizational change. I also learned that the directive approach (telling) will achieve only limited results.

A total of 18 lessons were learned, representing 100 percent of all lessons associated with this event. Fifteen of the thirty-three lessons were not reported by those managers who believed that Line-to-Staff Switches was a key event in their career progression.

Assignments Events Summary

The six assignments that played a key role in the career progression of these 78 SES women covered most major assignments within a department and ranged in positions from staff to line, from line to staff, from technician to manager, from specialist to generalist, from manager to SES, and from an "unsure of self" person to a self-confident leader. These were hands-on, developmental assignments; for the most part, the women learned as they did the assignment and found they could survive. It was stressful for most and fun for others. As they worked on the assignments, they faced many challenges. This work took an enormous amount of time, commitment, dedication, and sometimes risk. Each of the lessons associated with the event contributed to the women's banks of knowledge and made significant differences in their credibility and visibility. One woman executive summed up this journey of getting into the SES: "Everything you have learned comes into being."

OTHER PEOPLE CLUSTER

Other People was the next ranking category in contributing to the development of the 78 SES career women. This category consisted of two events: Bosses/Role Models and Values Played Out. The central point of this category was that people were the main event, not just a subsidiary to the development of the executive.

The Bosses/Role Models event encompassed many people who were involved in each woman's personal and professional life: families, husbands, children, subordinates, superiors, internal and external people, peers, professional groups, politicians, world leaders, managers, bosses, customers, the public, legislators, and others. This event was broad and went deeper than the knowledge of behaviors and the relationship of people to the task. Both bosses and role models contributed positive and negative experiences that could be used by the woman to manage, plan, and move in her career. Sometimes it was just a supportive word, and at other times there was special attention provided to the executive. Many of these relationships were longstanding, and some of the women relied upon these people for assistance and advice. The majority of these people were bosses; a number of other role models were mentioned as well.

The Values Played Out event refers to the values of the organization, the bosses, and sometimes the manager herself. Most of the time, this event was short-lived but stood out to the executive as having an impact on her in standing up for her beliefs.

Bosses/Role Models

N events = 47 (15.4 percent of all events)
N lessons = 198 (14.6 percent of all lessons)
N managers = 47 (60.2 percent of all managers)

This event was the most reported event by the executives; in fact, 60.2 percent of all respondents listed this as the most significant event in their careers in government. This category was defined as someone, usually a superior, whom the executive had interacted with, observed, or emulated during her career. This supportive boss/person "watched over her," provided her with opportunities, let her know about assignments, and introduced her to influential people. Some bosses' support led to other jobs, and some just gave her self-confidence. The negative model—observing management styles or game-playing tactics that the women could not support—was also an important learning tool. These bosses/role models, positive and negative, helped the woman learn how to manage herself, her projects, her staff, and her resources. Although most of the bosses/role models were men who played a key event in their careers, two women were singled out as well: Connie Newman, former OPM director, and Frances Perkins, former secretary of the Department of Labor. One woman described Perkins as her "all-time heroine." Another highly mentioned relationship that evolved in some of these experiences was having a mentor, defined as a boss or other person who guided them or pushed them into a position; 65.4 percent of the women said they had a mentor at some time in their career. The Bosses/Role Models key event was significant in many ways for these 78 SES career women.

I have had many people who influenced my style of management—managers I have worked under whose style I admired. I have had several mentors along the way who didn't have to do what they did.

I worked day-to-day with highly motivated, highly respected, talented, accomplished people. They became the norm of my world. These are the people I want to emulate.

Early in my career I used to watch my bosses and others in meetings, briefings, and other situations and think: "If I ever have to do that, I would handle it like he did" or in some cases, "If I ever had to do that, I certainly wouldn't do what he did." I wanted to know how to behave to get ahead, and I looked for good and bad approaches and made a point of remembering what worked and what didn't.

In this key event, the three most frequent lessons learned were All about How Government Works, Self-Confidence, and Management Models. Learning the system of the government—how it operates, its structure, its rules and regulations, and its power—was the most-reported lesson learned in this event.

> My first boss was an exemplary teacher with the highest standards of performance who taught me a lot about the ways of government and how to fit in successfully.

> I rode in a carpool with the head of an administrative section. Every day he would discuss personnel issues. He gave me reading assignments in the FPMs [Federal Personnel Manuals] and taught me how to learn the system. He would then quiz me about what I had read.

Self-Confidence encompassed trusting one's own competence, knowing one's strengths and weaknesses, taking risks, handling tough situations, and learning to be successful.

> There have been any number of special people during my career. Two are very significant to me. One mentored me [and] the other, a recent boss, readily shared his knowledge. In both instances, these individuals went out of their way to make me grow and become confident in my ability. Both pushed me very far and fast but were there for support when I needed them.

> She taught me the most; she put me in charge and let me do it and kept telling me, "I know you can do it."

Learning about Management Models was done through observing how others managed. The executives discussed how they learned management processes and theories from a boss or mentor.

> Even though I had many mentors, he was the one who carefully and strategically taught me how to make the transition to management. There were no women in major management positions, so I had to rely upon men for my mentoring. I studied them and the organization critically, observing what worked and why.

> Learned from good and bad managers some very basic principles. People like to be thanked. People like to be told in a non-confrontational way what is wrong [with their performance]. The way for me to look good is if

my people look good. Respect people for abilities and what they can do, not their education or their age.

[My boss] made me understand the benefits of a rigorous control and co-ordination system. I learned his approach to coordinate everything—don't let any stone go un-turned; keep all bases covered; and get input from everyone including political appointees—before the final paper was complete.

By watching another supervisor who didn't reward and recognize his peo-ple, I learned the importance of recognizing others. These differences shape you and determine how your staff reacts to you.

I watched other people manage. I learned how not to manage, learned how not to antagonize people, and how to get the most out of people.

The executives received valuable information from 31 of the 33 lessons learned from the Bosses/Role Model event. Fifteen of them composed 81.3 percent of the major lessons learned in this event. Two lessons were not experienced in this key event: Understanding Other People's Perspectives (Handling Relationships) and Personal Limits and Blind Spots (Personal Awareness) (Figure 5.3).

Values Played Out

N events = 9 (3 percent of all events)

N lessons = 31 (2.3 percent of all lessons)

N managers = 9 (11.5 percent of all managers)

The behaviors associated with the Values Played Out event were short-lived and occurred at work. The executives related anecdotes that usually happened in the past but were imprinted in their memory. All related in one way or another to the value system of the executive herself, her boss, or the organization. One ex-ecutive thought she had forgotten about the incident and did not realize how it had influenced her management style. Another discussed how everything else in her career always could be traced to how she had reacted to the behaviors asso-ciated with a particular manager in a certain situation. Many described their par-ticipation in reduction-in-force assignments (trying to put it in perspective), in reorganizations that required abolishing jobs and firing people (trying to be sen-sitive to people's lives), transferring or closing down projects that their staffs had worked on their whole professional life (costing taxpayer money without results or for political reasons), and the risks associated with not performing a particular task because of their own value system in treating people fairly and honestly.

Since my initial entry into employment, I have been impressed with the expectation that the bottom line matters; i.e., the number of contacts

Figure 5.3
Bosses/Role Models

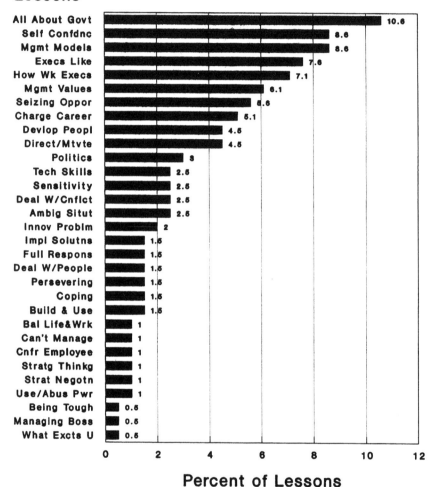

Lessons

All About Govt	10.6
Self Confdnc	8.6
Mgmt Models	8.6
Execs Like	7.6
How Wk Execs	7.1
Mgmt Values	6.1
Seizing Oppor	5.6
Charge Career	5.1
Devlop Peopl	4.6
Direct/Mtvte	4.6
Politics	3
Tech Skills	2.6
Sensitivity	2.6
Deal W/Cnflct	2.6
Ambig Situt	2.6
Innov Problm	2
Impl Solutns	1.6
Full Respons	1.6
Deal W/People	1.6
Persevering	1.6
Coping	1.6
Build & Use	1.6
Bal Life&Wrk	1
Can't Manage	1
Cnfr Employee	1
Stratg Thinkg	1
Strat Negotn	1
Use/Abus Pwr	1
Being Tough	0.6
Managing Boss	0.6
What Excts U	0.6

Percent of Lessons

Source: 1991 Survey of FED Women Executives by D. M. Little

which are made, the quality of the contacts which includes the satisfaction of the [client], and the cost at which the contacts are made.

This orientation [of working within your own value system] has continually influenced my management objectives and my management style. I have always tried to communicate to my subordinates this same expectation [the value that working together as a team was important to her] and to let them know that their development, satisfaction, and advancement will be largely determined by how well we as a team work to deliver a good bottom-line result.

When we were facing sequestration [budget] and furlough possibilities, I took these actions as serious. Others saw bodies and not people. I considered leaving the job because of these sequestration problems and their effect on the people.

Found myself in a job ideally suited for me, but with a boss who was not— different personal styles, outlooks, and values. Very frustrating. Learned that I'm not very good at establishing rapport with someone for whom I have no respect whatsoever—I'm good at it with people I don't like as long as they play fair and have a sincere commitment to their own sense of values.

I had frequent contact with an official that manipulated people to a degree. I saw him as a terrible example of a manager. I saw how people can be manipulated by higher levels, and I didn't want to be part of it. The system took care of him.

I wanted to send a message that these things would not be tolerated.

Within this event, Handling Political Situations was the most-cited lesson learned. It involved complex behavior that sometimes could not be explained through a vignette but sometimes was an overall impression on how the political system had its own values, and the career executive's job was to implement them. Sometimes the executive just said no; other times she went around the system; some did what was asked. Those women who provided Handling Political Situations as their key lesson remembered it vividly. Many discussed just the outcome of the lesson and what they had learned.

There are risks involved to stand up for your ethics. You work for yourself and what you think is right and you still stay with the organization but need to live with yourself. Things change overnight. Political appointees change and so do agency goals.

Hill staffer wanted me to spy and feed information to use in hearings. Refused and I was given retribution.

Worked on a project—White House, OPM, and State Department involved. I had to tell them "no." I do not believe that I had the authority to do it. I learned to know the parameters of my responsibilities. I am not refusing to help you, but I can't go beyond my authority. Know facts setting up the situation and sticking with it. If someone overrules you, you haven't lost face. Congress overturned the President.

There were four lessons that tied for second place: two in the Handling Relationships cluster (Directing and Motivating Employees and How to Work with Executives) and two in the Basic Values cluster (Sensitivity to the Human Side of Management and Basic Management Values). Because of the nature of these lessons learned, most of them dealing with people and being sensitive to them and treating them fairly, many executives learned from observing others' actions toward another person, usually in a hierarchical relationship. These behaviors were both positive and negative, and each lesson learned was an insight into how the woman executive applied that to her own management style.

> Environments are positive and negative. Learn from them and grow with the negative environments. Reductions in Force (RIF) bring out the worst in people and make them unproductive. Congress and President wanted to do away with a public function. It makes you question the values you come in with. You learn in negative situations that people are fragile.

> Didn't want to go along [with him]. Afraid I wouldn't be able to continue telling him he was wrong. Stressful.

> Sometimes he would withhold information. I quit worrying about this, because I felt if it was going to be wrong, someone would tell me. If it didn't need to be done that way, it would be apparent to me.

> I had to stand up for what I believed in. I learned to be sensitive to the person and the position.

> How people were treated was not in accord with my value system. I had a hard time dealing with [x].

Although these were short episodes, many of these Values Played Out scenarios were very visible within the organization and sometimes throughout the federal government. The women had this advice regarding their values based on these experiences:

> Do unto others as you would have them do unto you. If you think about managers you have had that made you feel good or bad and apply these same standards to those who work for you.

> Everything is not always black and white.

> Learn to maintain your integrity. What goes around comes around.

> Know the value systems within an organization, and understand its role.

> Keep a sense of perspective in dealing with the public; you've got to be reasonable. People have motivation to follow the rules.

> When you are wrong, promptly admit it.

Eighteen lessons represented 100 percent of the Values Playing Out event. There were 15 lessons not learned within this event: 3 within Setting and Implementing Agendas, 5 within Handling Relationships, 1 within Basic Values, 1 within Executive Temperament, and 5 within Personal Awareness.

Other People Summary

In Bosses/Role Models and Values Playing Out, the main focus was observing others and their actions and behaviors in organizations. Both positive and negative experiences played a part in formulating the behaviors of the women who learned, through these two events, how to manage their career and to be successful. The women learned by watching others, interpreting the information, and incorporating this knowledge into their own management portfolios. The importance of these two events was traced in the career progression of these 78 SES career women.

HARDSHIPS CLUSTER

Five key events fall in this category: Career Setback, Changing Jobs, Personal Trauma, Employee Performance Problems, and Organizational Mistakes. These events had negative connotations, yet positive rewards emerged from the experiences. These women grew to know themselves, to understand what they wanted, and to recognize their limits. In these five events, the women themselves were the focus. They faced career setbacks, job changes, personal trauma, employee performance problems, and organizational mistakes. How they coped was evidenced through the lessons they learned, wide-ranging ones that covered a broad range of experiences. There was no particular time in their careers when they had this experience; for some it was early, some middle, and some in the SES. Many considered the experience a personal challenge and survived it; others left the position or were forced out. But most of the women emerged with confidence in herself as a person and as a manager. All 78 SES career women at one time or another experienced one or more of these events in their careers.

Changing Jobs

N events = 24 (7.9 percent of all events)

N lessons = 117 (8.6 percent of all lessons)

N managers = 24 (30.1 percent of all managers)

The Changing Jobs event was the highest reported event in the Hardships category. Of all lessons learned by the 16 events of the study, this contained 8.6 percent of all lessons. This event was not just about changing careers but also was a planned change in jobs by the executive. They chose to leave their previous position for a new opportunity: going back to school, changing agencies, moving to another field, taking a downgrade, leaving government, or coming to government. The reasons to take the risk of changing jobs varied, but two were reported most frequently: job boredom or a discontentment with their job and/or the people they worked with. The women needed new challenges and opportunities; some wanted to see if they could do something different. Learning new fields, meeting new people, starting with a clean slate, and working with a fresh approach were a few benefits of taking the plunge to change jobs and start anew.

> I felt I needed to move at this career point and try something different or I would be here forever.

> Job opened up as program analyst (cost financial analysis for programs). It was a big change in terms of career pattern and experience.

> Moved to a new field as a GS-12. Good move regarding future growth.

The top-ranking lesson emerging from this event was learning All about How Government Works. Understanding the system of government was important in changing positions and a major milestone in the success of the executive in the new job.

> I went from [one agency to another] to give myself an opportunity to work with a different echelon of people—political appointees. It helped to broaden my understanding of how government worked; it gave me visibility with political appointees.

> Came to government [to work on a special project]. I am learning to use my private-sector experience.

> Moved from a defense to a non-defense agency. I made a conscious decision to move. It took a year to make the move. Felt like I had moved from one government to another government—difference in functions and culture. It was a broadening of horizons. Exposed to politics of government and the reality. Went through a cultural shock. Learned so many different ways to do things and to do them effectively. Need to remain open and recognize lots of options.

> I left a research position to enter government. In government carried along by events; constant deadlines; very interactive with others. Always part of an interrelated structure and must deal with it. Everything different from research where you are on your own, self-motivated, and self-driven.

Also ranking high was the Technical/Professional Skills lesson.

Volunteered for a grunt assignment to be a servicing personnel specialist. Learned the system. I showed I was willing to take on assignments. I had a group leader position; I moved to a program area; I kept increasing my responsibility. As I focused on my career, I took an assignment in a policy office (a ticket to punch at the 14 level), then I moved to a deputy job managing 50 subordinates. I then took a lateral move (needed to punch ticket) in order to accomplish my long-range goals.

Made a conscious decision to ask to go in an operating personnel office. I had to play catch-up.

I made lemonade out of a lemon. [I kept saying] a public career is worth it. I changed cultures to energize myself and to know another area. I shifted gears, and it was rewarding.

The next five lessons were equal in distribution for this event. Three of the lessons were in the Executive Temperament cluster (Self-Confidence, Coping with Ambiguous Situations, and Coping with Situations beyond Your Control), one lesson was in Basic Values (Sensitivity to the Human Side of Management), and one was in Personal Awareness (Recognizing and Seizing Opportunities).

Took a political appointee job at the state and local level. Having to deal with policy agenda and public policy was a different approach for me. I had dealt with career people all my life, so this was a little different. It gave me a sense of and an opportunity to understand what it is to be in the public eye. It gave me a different perspective and sensitivity of what is required to be a political appointee.

Moving from one substantive area to another, I learned the value of versatility.

A White House initiative was brought to my attention. I looked at the design of the program and wanted to go and implement the program. I asked and received a leave of absence for two years. I always believed that if you treat people differently and nurture them and expect them to be successful they will succeed. [From this project], I proved this to be true.

I left the personnel field for a data systems job. An all-involved job change—a change in scope of management and different technical and management levels.

I took myself out of the fast track.

I readily accepted an assignment to positions about which I knew very little, learned about them and performed in a manner which made me a logical choice for promotion to a more responsible position. From making moves of this kind, I have gained confidence in myself that I can conquer new areas of responsibility, perform well, and have an impact.

I accepted a political appointee position. This shaped my behavior.

Came to government from a large corporation. I wanted a job with less travel to foreign countries. Wanted to maximize what I like.

There were 24 managers who described their experiences in Changing Jobs, the only event of the 16 that had all 33 lessons learned. It also contained the most number of lessons learned within the 75 percent cumulative range. Because of tied lessons, the actual percentage was 82.9 percent (Figure 5.4).

Career Setback

N events = 12 (3.9 percent of all events)
N lessons = 52 (3.8 percent of all lessons)
N managers = 12 (15.4 percent of all managers)

The Career Setback event was about crisis situations, lousy jobs, demotions, and missed promotions. These events were usually forced upon the executive; she had no choice but to leave her position or to remain in it. This forced-out event occurred when the executive took a stance or made a personal mistake, or there was a change in administration, reorganization, new boss, new programs, transfer of function, or a difference of philosophy. For the missed promotions, the women felt disgraced and depressed. In each case they had to think about themselves: what they can do, who they are, and where and how to restart their lives. These were trying and challenging times.

I had held for three years the number three position in [the agency] supervising agency-wide personnel, budgeting, administrative services, finance, and data systems. I got along well with my immediate boss. A new [boss] was appointed and confirmed, and I only worked with him a couple of weeks before going on two-months' maternity leave. Two months after I returned, he reassigned me to another job [with less status]. Before I [went to the job], the guys had closed ranks to cut me out of any action. For 18 months the highlight of my day was when someone put something in my in-box to read. I had a few GS-12–level projects but had to really search to find things to do. I was depressed the whole time I was in that job. It was the low point of my career; I felt I was in disgrace. I learned who my friends were (the ones who kept in touch) and how important it is to support other executives, male and female, who run afoul of whatever situations might be out of their control.

Figure 5.4
Changing Jobs

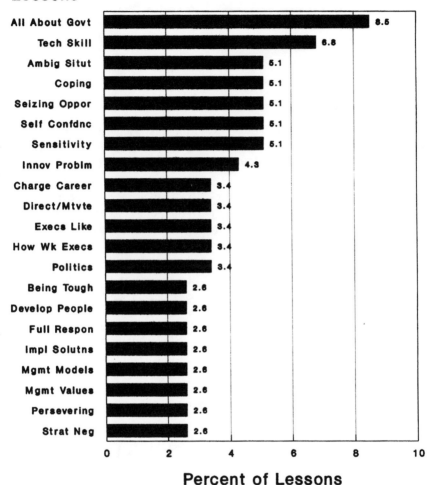

Lessons

Lesson	Percent
All About Govt	8.5
Tech Skill	6.8
Ambig Situt	5.1
Coping	5.1
Seizing Oppor	5.1
Self Confdnc	5.1
Sensitivity	5.1
Innov Problm	4.3
Charge Career	3.4
Direct/Mtvte	3.4
Execs Like	3.4
How Wk Execs	3.4
Politics	3.4
Being Tough	2.6
Develop People	2.6
Full Respon	2.6
Impl Solutns	2.6
Mgmt Models	2.6
Mgmt Values	2.6
Persevering	2.6
Strat Neg	2.6

Percent of Lessons

Source: 1991 Survey of FED Women Executives by D. M. Little

I was sacked. I learned that I couldn't depend on boss's support when boss didn't hire me. I had always worked for boss who hired me. I learned to move when boss moves.

My supervisor was threatened by me and jealous. He started a conflict with me. First thing he did was he removed my staff, space, and work. It was fruitless to complain.

The lesson most learned here was Persevering through Adversity; 15.4 percent of the women said they had learned this lesson from this event. They found ways to overcome the obstacles, usually through hard work and an assessment of who they were and what they wanted to do about the situation.

> I was reassigned out of the program involuntarily. I was able to negotiate a better position. Learned to be straightforward and up-front and not to confuse the issues.

> [Key event] being moved. I learned some people only care about appearances and not about quality.

Coping with Situations beyond Your Control ranked almost as high (13.5 percent). In this lesson the women recognized they were operating under unrealistic expectations and dealing with uncontrollable environments.

> [After a training program, came back to work in agency.] All people who supported me had left, and the new [person] told my boss to get rid of me. For ten months I was ostracized by my organization and black-balled from other programs. It was a difficult time. I wasn't even allowed to attend staff meetings.

> Left last job—things not going well with boss. I had to leave the job. I thought I had a job, and it did not pan out. Learned don't make enemies, and don't take things personally.

> I became the acting director for a year. The "x" would not allow me to be the director, because I was not technical. Science community wanted me to be the director. It was upsetting at the time.

Although the setback was difficult, it helped them learn the third lesson: Taking Charge of Your Career.

> I learned something personally. I knew I could not work for someone who had a character disorder or was extremely neurotic. People who pit people against one another are so destructive. It creates a devastating effect. It impacts everyone. I found the job intolerable and left. What I learned is how not to manage and supervise.

> They gave me the GM-15 but parked me. Boss told me people were jealous of me—"So competent you overwhelm the opposition." I still didn't believe people were jealous of me. Boss said I must face up to it.

> I applied for two branch chief jobs and did not get them. First time I had to deal with this. I got depressed. It was an ego deflator. It affected my interest in having a branch chief job. Now see it was a good move [not to get the jobs].

Felt I was qualified [for the position]. When not selected, had to recast self in many ways. Had to figure out my experiences and skills and ask what kind of jobs could I do. It changed how I viewed myself.

I applied for a job and wasn't selected for it. It challenged my perception of myself (how good I am) and my self-esteem. It strengthened me in many ways. It forced me to face what I thought of myself. I had to be bedrock solid of that so I could maintain my own course and value myself.

Ten of the eighteen lessons reported learned in this event composed 84.5 percent of the total. There were also 15 lessons not reported by the executives in this event.

Employee Performance Problems

N events = 9 (3 percent of all events)

N lessons = 31 (2.3 percent of all lessons)

N managers = 9 (11.5 percent of all managers)

The Employee Performance Problems event was the least-described event by the executives. They were willing to share the information but cautious in relating the specific details because of privacy concerns. The red tape of the performance system was discussed. Many of the respondents had grievances, civil suits, equal employment opportunity (EEO) complaints, and administrative actions filed against them based on their actions. In many of these cases, it was a very emotional process that resulted in many long hours of deliberation to do the action, and, when committed to do it, to ensure it was done right. People outside government usually believe that the government does not fire people, but more than 10 percent of these respondents were responsible for firing someone for nonperformance. All of these problems were performance related. They were not personality conflicts or misunderstandings but significant enough for the executive to confront the employee and to try to take corrective action—counseling, training, or job rotation. All of the women considered their options and wrestled with the humane way to terminate the employee. Some people were transferred, but many of them were fired or retired.

[First job] needed to hold people accountable for their performance and not take easy way out. I learned being nice is not always appropriate. One should always be nice, but just being nice may not produce quality of work needed.

A totally ineffective person was assigned to work for me.

Grievances filed by subordinates. Learned some people are never satisfied.

The top lesson (22.5 percent) learned in this event was Confronting Employee Performance Problems. Many of the women reported that it took longer for them to strategize how to confront the person or the administrative process took more time than anticipated. If they had moved faster, the situation may not have damaged the organization as much and may not have been such an emotional and draining experience.

A secretary was abusing leave, and I had to issue her a letter of warning about it. Another employee, a trainee, wanted to know why nothing happened to her. I explained to him that the disciplined employee had a right to privacy and that action had been taken. I learned that employees do not trust management to do the right thing. It is important to protect the employee's right to privacy, especially about disciplinary matters.

Denied annual leave, person went AWOL, I had to work until 10:00 at night and weekends to complete [contracts]. I went unprepared [to a meeting involving over 50 countries]. I got tired of being tough.

I had to take an adverse action against an employee. It was very difficult not only personally but professionally.

Did not tell someone they're not performing up to par.

A grievance was filed against me. I learned to figure out what you want your ultimate outcome to be. Don't let details get in your way. It taught me how difficult communications really are within large organizations. Organizations have set ways to settle disputes. Employee wanted something that I couldn't give her; neither could I get it. I had tried to solve the problem informally, and it was shocking to discover the employee had filed the grievance.

I had been promoted to my first line manager position from within the unit and was supervising my previous peers—not an easy transition. I was at least 20 years younger than any of the members. I counseled a 55 year old male about his performance, something which had never been done apparently. I did this in a very candid, but I thought, humane manner. Suddenly he was in tears, and I was quite disconcerted. The ultimate outcome of the discussion was that he set his retirement date.

I learned that an employee who I presumed to be fully loyal and who I'd found very likeable—though I'd commenced to wonder about his level of competence—was in fact seriously disloyal. He was doing damage to the organization and to me personally. I set matters to right, but at some cost. What I learned was to be less naive, less trusting, and thereafter more vigilant. A splendid personality can hide a multitude of sins, and greater caution than I'd been accustomed to exercising is crucial.

The next three lessons ranked 12.9 percent and concerned learning about being tough and taking the action (Being Tough When Necessary), learning how to cope with situations that you cannot control once the action begins (Coping with Situations beyond Your Control), and learning about how you would want to be treated in this situation (Sensitivity to the Human Side of Management).

[Person was not performing]. I built case to fire him and succeeded. Because of a technical error, he was reinstated. I could not supervise him.

An EEO complaint was filed against me. It came out of the blue, and I had no idea or even thought that people would consider that I would discriminate. I learned a lot from that crisis in terms of how I managed. I learned to keep people informed and apprised and to do a lot more reaching out to subordinates.

Hardest thing for me to do was to go to Middle East to fire employees who were stealing from the organization. It was emotionally difficult.

People were not performing, I had to fire them. It was all-encompassing and consuming; felt awful; upset; worst thing I have ever had to do.

Dealing with an alcoholic subordinate was extremely difficult. I also find it difficult to deal with subordinates who frame everything in terms of personal identity; i.e., constructive feedback, however given, is taken as a personal attack rather than viewed as a performance issue. I have had to remove both top-level managers and subordinate executives from their positions, and this is never a pleasant situation. I hope I never live long enough to enjoy it.

In my first supervisory job, I was in the job for six months. I had to fire someone. It was very painful, and I had a terrible Thanksgiving. I learned to hang together and get promises from everyone before you go out on a limb to take the action.

There were 14 lessons learned in the Employee Performance Problems event, representing 100 percent of the lessons. Nineteen lessons were not part of this event.

Organizational Mistakes

N events = 6 (2 percent of all events)

N lessons = 28 (2.1 percent of all lessons)

N managers = 6 (7.7 percent of all managers)

Organizational Mistakes were just that: internal organizational mistakes that slowed the executives' career progress. In most instances, the women were quick bouncers; they took the issue in hand and made solutions work. Most of these errors fell within the realm of inexperience, being new to the job, or not knowing the system. Sometimes the executive overstepped her authority and was too impulsive, making decisions without all the information; other times she kept all the cards to herself and did not keep higher-level people informed. In some cases, the woman thought she might be fired but used her management skills to rectify the situation.

> I learned from my mistakes, because I didn't delegate to others.

> I signed an agreement without approval.

> Had responsibility for all the work. I had misread the cues. Thought I would be fired. I learned I needed to figure out how to face up and stay and correct it.

The executives reported that the lessons of Coping with Situations beyond Your Control, Being Tough When Necessary (Executive Temperaments), and Handling Political Situations (Handling Relationships) were learned in the Organizational Mistakes event.

> I made a mistake. I called husband and told him I was going to jump out of the window. I was able to correct the mistake and was also able to admit the mistake in front of high-level executives.

> My fault for failing to clear "politically."

> Was given a project and I needed to get consensus of [everyone] and couldn't. I dropped the ball, and it was visible.

> Had an agenda which was to abolish the functions and to downsize. I didn't pick up on this. What they said was not what they did. My staff was moved. They operated with fast action and didn't want it to be co-opted. Never realized the morale damage. Felt inadequate as a manager. Couldn't tell the ax was falling, because I just didn't know.

Although 19 lessons (100 percent) were reported as learned within this event, 13 of them received the same rating of 3.6 percent. Fourteen lessons were not reported as learned in this event.

Personal Trauma

N events = 5 (1.5 percent of all events)

N lessons = 16 (1.2 percent of all lessons)

N managers = 5 (6.4 percent of all managers)

Personal Trauma involved an emotional crisis that occurred to the individual herself or to her family. These tragedies made the executive stop and think about her life and how she wanted to live it. Several changed their approach to management and used the experience to be more sensitive to others and their problems. Others are still trying to cope and hope they will survive the problem or at least that it will not affect their work.

After a long illness and death of a family member, it made me more sympathetic to employees. Made me more human.

These lessons were all in the Personal Awareness cluster: Balance between Work and Personal Life, Taking Charge of Your Career, and Recognizing and Seizing Opportunities. Within these three lessons was a common thread, a need to take charge of one's life and seize every opportunity to live life to its fullest.

Living with death. Living more today.

Trying not to let a family illness [and death] affect my work in a significant way.

After a car accident I was told I was permanently totally disabled (and only 35!). [Learned to be independent.]

At 11, my mother committed suicide, and I had to take care of the family.

Divorce was mentioned by many of the women in this study, but none said it was a key event in their careers. Many had gone through divorce, and 5 percent of the executives were separated or in divorce proceedings. Several executives mentioned the emotional aspect of the divorce and what they had learned about themselves from such an emotional experience. Their comments varied:

I've made the most big growth when I had the support of a mate. I got into trouble when I was alone—no one to talk to, to provide psychological support.

Freedom to relocate geographically and travel extensively have contributed to my success and growth as a manager.

I can now work late without feeling guilty.

I don't have to worry about being more successful than my husband.

I can devote more time to my job.

I am free to travel more and be mobile.

Although 11 lessons were learned by having this event in their careers, 22 lessons were not learned—the highest number of lessons not learned for any of the 16 events.

Hardships Summary

The crises that happened in the career lives of these 78 women were very personal experiences. Many careers were made based upon how the woman reacted to these events, which took up enormous amounts of time and were stressful and draining. In each event, the executive had to confront herself and ask questions about her behavior. Except for the Personal Trauma event, the events took place after the executive was in a working environment, with most events occurring later in her career (GS-13 and above). How they learned from each of the events and applied the lessons to the situation were largely up to them. The reaction to and the outcome of these hardships made differences in the career progression of the women.

OTHER EVENTS CLUSTER

Three events did not seem to fit any other category; they nevertheless represented a large number of lessons women learned and helped the women move up the career ladder. Presented in rank order of significance reported by the women, they are Coursework, Early Work Experience, and Purely Personal. There were no common threads running through these three lessons; they occurred at work and outside and at different times during the executives' work career.

Coursework

N events = 26 (8.5 percent of all events)

N lessons = 71 (5.2 percent of all lessons)

N managers = 26 (33 percent of all managers)

Coursework encompasses formal academic programs and intern or development programs. The academic and formal education programs—long- and short-term university programs, nonuniversity programs, and in-house programs—provided the manager with opportunities to explore many diverse topics in an off-site environment. In the formal intern or development programs, the manager was exposed to many high-level people, different offices, varied functions, and diverse occupations. In both types of training, the manager acquired information that she could not have gained in her present position. Except for the Ph.D. and professional (law and medicine) degrees, the opportunities to go to these training programs were provided and supported by the federal government. Several of the executives had left government to work toward a degree that was required for credentials in their specialty field; law and science were most frequently mentioned.

> Went to law school. Taught me to be more theoretical, analyze problems faster and to look at all aspects of them.

Forty-one percent of the respondents attended the four-week or seven-week programs of the Federal Executive Institute (FEI). One executive summed up many of the others' comments regarding their experience: "I enjoyed FEI because of it being residential, and I had a chance to exchange thoughts and issues." Only two executives reported it as a key event in their careers. Several executives discussed short, nonuniversity courses that had made a difference; public speaking ranked the highest. Eight executives had attended the 3-week (Senior Managers in Government), 13-week (Senior Executive Fellows), or 10-month (Mid-Career Masters in Public Administration) programs at Harvard. One woman had attended Simmons Graduate School of Management, another the National War College.

Several formal intern or development programs—Management Intern Program, Presidential Management Intern, and internal agency programs—had influenced the managers' behaviors. Many of them occurred early in their career. The one most reported at the upper end of their career (GM-14 and GM-15) was the Senior Executive Service Candidate Development Program (SESCDP). Several women had participated in the President's Executive Exchange Program. In each program there were competency instructions, observation of high-level managers, assignments, and exposure to various ways of managing.

The formal intern programs were all encompassing as far as exposure to the management models and process, high-level executives, and the government system. The top-ranked lesson learned in this event, at 23.9 percent, was Management Models. Most of the executives reported that the opportunity to be in a formal educational program was a key event in knowing about and applying management principles and observing others.

> Went on a Congressional Fellowship and spent one and a half years on the Hill. It opened my eyes on what was happening in town. Thrown into many areas I knew nothing about. Did it all. I saw all the issues, got direct feedback and didn't have many levels to go through. Also, selected by another department for their SESCDP program. I received excellent help. It was in an area I knew nothing about. I am sorry I had not chosen [this field] earlier. People were held accountable, and the mission was more urgent. It was action-oriented, and people knew more about what they were doing.

> I was in the Management Intern Program and rotated through different programs at beginning of my career. Many significant people came in

through this vehicle, probably more men than women. People who were in this program were pegged as having brains. Learned how to be flexible.

Selected into the "New Blood Intern Program." I learned all about the budget business.

Was in a 2 year internal Agency Federal Intern Program that taught all of the personnel functions. Had opportunity to get experience at OPM (3 month assignment) and HHS [Department of Health and Human Services]. I built a relationship in the intern program and created a network to talk to.

Was rotated in an internal agency program. Learned from courses how to and how not to manage. I learned to recognize people have different personalities and to react accordingly. It made me more sensitive to others.

Self-Confidence was the second-ranked lesson (14.1 percent) learned in this event. Both academic and intern programs provided the executive with credentials (formal and informal) to show that she could do a job and be a productive and valued asset to the government.

Received Ph.D. and it gave me confidence and now could take place as a scientist. In agency of scientists and engineers must have Ph.D. to be credentialed.

Took a Public Speaking course; it helped me to do a better job and gave me confidence.

High on learning. See self as a perpetual student. Attended LEGIS [LEGIS (Legislative) Fellows Program], SESCDP, and PEEP [President Executive Exchange Program]. Support education and training programs.

University programs were taken primarily to get credentials in a specific technical area. The Technical/Professional Skills lesson was reported in the top three lessons (12.7 percent) learned in this event.

Went to law school. Taught me to be more theoretical, analyze problems faster and to look at all aspects of it.

Attended the 3-week Harvard Senior Managers program. In 1985, I went to Harvard for a Master's in Public Administration. Learned to get my priorities straight.

First woman to get Ph.D. at MIT. Learned my technical specialty.

Went to the 10-month Mid-Career program at Harvard. Received my MPA. Education is important. I feel you can't have too much education. People are very credential-oriented.

Prior to law school I worked at various jobs. After law degree, it put me into the category of lawyers.

Went to Harvard Senior Management Program (3 weeks). I came away with learning a lot. Through application envisage myself on a balcony and step back sometimes and see what is happening, because when you are in [the issue] you can't see it. I haven't mastered all these things, but they have influenced how I manage today.

I took a course on how to manage change. It did a great job in turning staff around. I got more loyalty from the people. My people strengths got stronger.

Did Master's work at University of Michigan. Learned to network and seek out the people of leadership.

Master's Degree in Public Administration at USC [University of Southern California] gave me a conceptual framework of government and showed me the kind of people I wanted to be with. I learned respect for people. It gave me a critical intervention. It gave me different dimensions and a lifetime profession. It inspired me to spend life in public service.

Getting Ph.D. was important. It taught me the need to persevere and to finish. I felt there was value in this process. Learned how to coordinate with others.

Short- and long-term nonuniversity courses also played a large role in helping the executive learn. Three other lessons were learned in this event: Recognizing and Seizing Opportunities (9.9 percent), Taking Charge of Your Career (8.5 percent), and All about How Government Works (7 percent).

Took advanced management training—management of scientists and engineers and American Management Association middle management course. Learned.

Essential to understand what motivates individuals—their values. Any system or technique that ignores this will fail to yield desired results.

Trained to death. Thought I knew everything, but I learned a lot about new management training. The training made me more secure in what I did and what I knew. FEI helped me to change. Had not had management training until then.

Took a course, Advanced Management for Government Executives, at USDAGS [U.S. Department of Agriculture Graduate School]. I liked the structure—one day, one week (Virginia Beach), and 1 to 3 months later had follow-up sessions. Between Virginia Beach and the follow-up had opportunity to apply what I learned. The concept of barriers was discussed.

Came back and wanted to do one thing they recommended and that was face desk to wall. I didn't think I would like it. After a couple of months instead of my desk as a barrier, I felt it presented a different feeling; I felt people were more open and free and more capable of dealing with the issue. It made a change in how people related to me.

Attended National War College. Not only was this experience beneficial in terms of broadening my personal knowledge and experience base, but it was also an important "ticket" to be punched in my career progression.

Attended a one-week seminar; it was an intensified management behavior seminar. Course focused on style and behavior, and I received feedback on how I was perceived. I learned I came across too strong and overpowering.

Attended the Advanced Managers Workshop and went there as a GS-14, and it was for GS-15's. During a problem-solving exercise, I had the highest score, but group ignored it. Was told they aren't going to let you lead because you are a woman. Group started voting and stopped listening to me. People voted for boss who wouldn't rock the boat. I didn't have the early sense that I was supposed to play dumb. I learned to look at the world as a common denominator. There are A's and C's in the world and shouldn't strive to be the best.

The Treasury Executive Institute helped me get valuable leadership training.

I took a supervisory course to help me learn about managing people, how one motivates people, and techniques for dealing with people. Learned about conflict resolution.

The Center for Creative Leadership (CCL) course, "Leadership at the Peak," was crucial for me. [It was reinforcing and a confidence builder.]

Went to CCL program and to the Harvard School of Management. I never went through the "stations of the cross." Learned about negotiations skills, importance of building alliances, team work, and saw how to get there without being stuck in the small stuff. Figure out what you want and who you are. Learned to fill in some blanks about myself and to learn about strategic thinking.

Because of its importance as a feeder into the Senior Executive Service, the SESCDP, which has a formally announced selection process consisting of assessment centers and interviews, has been separated from the formal intern programs. Ten executives participated in these programs, which varied in content and length as determined by their agency; all of them provided the executives with information not available on a day-to-day basis. Some of these were listed as key events in their career; without this experience, some of the women probably would not have made it into the SES.

I was hired into an SESCDP at an agency where I was not an employee. It was a two-year development program where I worked in many areas. I also got to attend management courses at the University of Pennsylvania and the Michigan Program. I learned a lot in the classroom. I found it helpful to go to different organizations. It was an interesting educational experience—learned to strategize.

I was selected into the formal SESCDP program. I took advantage of the program. I found out my strengths and weaknesses and used it to try out different things—(1) tried out staff support, (2) looked for rotational assignments in line organization—procurement (supervised 75 people), (3) tried senior specialist, supervised 150 people, and (4) spent time looking at self and learning on the job activities.

As a GS-14 selected into the SESCDP. I had never been a manager before. I liked the newness. Learned to be more technical regarding budget and resource allocation.

I applied and got into the SESCDP program. I had to take a 3-month assignment in New York (had an 18 month and 4 year old at home and left them while on assignment). I never focused on making excuses for not doing it. I did learn to balance work and personal life.

Got good training at the [agency's] SESCDP. It was good training. Got to read management and supervisory books.

Two executives discussed their sabbaticals as a learning process, but only one listed it as a key event that had helped her as a manager.

There were many ways to learn in this event, and some were reported while discussing other key events: going to conventions, joining professional associations (one executive believed her status in the professional association helped protect her, and she was able to be more outspoken in her position), and reading books, trade journals, and news magazines.

Other courses stood out for the executives: public speaking (the most-cited skill, important to know how to give briefings and speeches), Outward Bound, Managing with Effectiveness, OPM Executive Seminar Centers, George Washington Continuing Executive Development Program, leadership, and human relations. Two executives discussed their own agencies' senior management programs; two others described their agencies' specific intern programs. All saw these programs as useful in their career progression:

Training is important; need to be involved in developmental assignments; it helps you look beyond your immediate environment. Adaptability is required. What is a challenge is to reconcile one's learning with the realities that one has to handle on a day-to-day basis.

The six lessons discussed represented 76.1 percent of the total lessons learned. There were 15 lessons not learned through this event (Figure 5.5).

Early Work Experience

N events = 19 (6.2 percent of all events)
N lessons = 75 (5.5 percent of all lessons)
N managers = 19 (24.5 percent of all managers)

Early Work Experiences were events that took place early in the SES women's careers, primarily before the women started their federal government careers. For some, the event was their first job; for others, it was a turning point in their careers. The learned lessons were varied and encompassed the five major lesson cluster groups: Setting and Implementing Agendas, Handling Relationships, Basic Values, Executive Temperament, and Personal Awareness.

> Worked on Hill for a Senator. Being on the Hill was fun—subject interesting, boss interesting, everyone young and college-educated. You get a bit of identity when you work for a political figure. Gives you an entirely different perspective. You get to do things not normally available.

> Early in my teens, leadership skills were nurtured in after-school activities—resulting in a year of college spent abroad in leadership training.

The top two lessons reported in this event were All about How Government Works and Professional/Technical Skills. These positions helped the executive learn the importance of making something happen and of having professional and technical skills.

> I baby sat for the Vice President of [the university I attended]. I consciously took the job so I could get to know, watch, and talk to him. I asked for his thought processes and learned a lot [about leadership and the ways to get things done].

> Waitressing taught me many things: pay for performance, know how to sell, learn the system and how to make it work for me, and helped me understand people.

> I launched my career by taking the FSEE [Federal Service Entrance Examination] to get into a professional position. It was a turning point, and I wanted to stay in Federal Government.

> I volunteered to work on a political campaign. I like the camaraderie of it. Felt satisfaction working hard for a common goal and had a real project to work on.

Figure 5.5
Coursework

Lessons

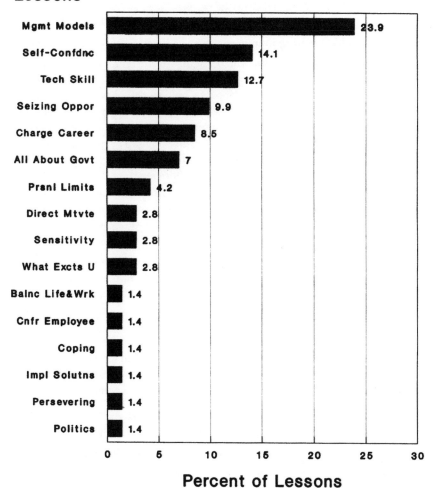

Percent of Lessons

Source: 1991 Survey of FED Women Executives by D. M. Little

Had an impossible time getting job. Turned down and told company did not hire women. Hired to research urban centers. Tried to gather data in hostile neighborhoods. [I was] totally responsible for work produced [at the research center].

Organized conference for research corporation (non-profit). I learned by doing it.

I met all the fine women on the President's Commission on the Status of Women. I had access to all the Big Wheels. Every day was exciting. From each one I learned something.

Four other lessons ranked in third place:

Directing and Motivating Employees

Serving as staff to a supervisor who constantly checked on me and yelled over the divider. This man seemed unable to delegate and let one work on a project. I am probably one of the most terrible workaholics that exist, and the constant checking irritated me no end. Also the yelling over the divider was demeaning. I learned to make assignments and then let people pursue them, checking only at strategic times to ensure that the project was still on track and to see if there was anything the individual needed from me. I approached it not on a checking basis but "is there anything I need to do to facilitate the process." I also always try to put myself in the shoes of the receiving individual to ground truth into my communications with staff. If one treats adults like children, they will end up resenting you and their job instead of being a productive, mature employee.

I had experience in a summer job while I was in college where I was a hostess in a restaurant with male waiters who were older than I. I used this experience.

How to Work with Executives

First job out of college volunteered to help set up a conference. I ended up in charge. Learned that even senior people often don't know how to do things, and a willingness to do something no one else wants to do impresses managers. It's easy to look successful (no one to compare to).

Dealing with People over Whom You Have No Authority

Responsible for a Neighborhood House, had small staff. Did everything—worked with community and government—helped people cope with realities of life and did fund raising for the program. [Learned how the system worked.]

Worked with dying patients as a Red Cross volunteer. I learned how to deal with people. People are the most important product we have.

Self-Confidence

[My husband] decided that I would run for the Council seat. At first I refused, but then I got so mad at the County Commissioners when they said, "You are going to get an airport whether you like it or not," that I told my husband, "maybe I will run!" I ran and beat my two opponents. In addition to self confidence and public speaking ability, I learned to talk to a variety of people, some of whom were angry about an issue, some of whom had views directly opposite from mine, some of whom were rude or derogatory, some of whom wanted information I did not have. I improved my ability to deal with people. I also improved my ability to set priorities.

In this event, 12 lessons comprised the top 75 percent of the lessons learned. From those women who described their early work experience, a total of 28 lessons were reported. They represented a variety of lessons. Five lessons were not reported: Use and Abuse of Power, Personal Limits and Blind Spots, Confronting Employee Performance Problems, Being Tough When Necessary, and Balance between Work and Personal Life.

Purely Personal

N events = 6 (2 percent of all events)

N lessons = 21 (1.5 percent of all lessons)

N managers = 6 (7.7 percent of all managers)

The Purely Personal event refers to one that usually shaped the executive in how she managed her career but in some instances her whole life. Although it had relevance to work, the experience usually occurred outside work and involved other people. It was a longstanding memory that stood out and a very personal and individual event.

I am a second generation American. I was taught if you study and get good grades you can be President. There is a residual feeling.

There were three lessons learned in this event that were significant: Balance between Work and Personal Life, Dealing with People over Whom You Have No Authority, and Taking Charge of Your Career.

As a Type A personality, I am a workaholic. As a child, I grew up in a Minister's home; so we constantly knew there was a professional daddy and a home daddy. This balance has helped.

Decided to adopt a child. I used to stay forever at work; now I manage differently to handle both parts of my life.

Work not good enough for boss; tried to commit suicide.

[I worked for my father.] He was a tough boss, especially on me; because I had to set a good example as the boss's daughter. I remember him saying that if I weren't at work on time, how could he get after anyone else for being late. He instilled good work habits in me early.

Thirteen other lessons were found in this event as reported by the women, but only one occurrence was reported in each—less than what could be expected from chance. Seventeen lessons were not covered in this event.

Other Events Summary

Three events—Coursework, Early Work Experience, and Purely Personal—were part of the formation of the executive's foundation of a career. Most of the events occurred early in their lives, and some of the lessons remain valid to their lives today. Although many of the lessons learned in the Coursework event were early in their careers, the executives have continued in a learning mode. The wide range of experiences and their importance in shaping the women's careers were the main common threads running through these events.

6

Getting Help from Others

Families, husbands, children, bosses, teachers, professors, subordinates, superiors, political appointees, mentors, supervisors, priests, ministers, co-workers, peers, professional acquaintances, friends, plus others too numerous to name played prominent roles in the career progression of these women. Some of them were supportive; some of them provided inspiration; some literally dragged them; some pulled them from the group; some handpicked them; some mentored them; some led them and showed them the way; some helped them find self-confidence; some found them a job or gave them promotions; some provided constructive feedback; some created a job for them; some paved the way for them; some were there when needed; and some made time for them. All in all, the people domain was the most important factor in the careers of these 78 SES women.

BOSSES/ROLE MODELS

The Bosses/Role Models event was the most-reported one, with 60.2 percent of all respondents listing this as the most significant event influencing their careers in government. The most important function of the boss and role model was to provide the behaviors in which the women could observe and decide what or if they could use this information. The learning took place through observing others. Both positive and negative behaviors were learned and stored in memory, to be brought forth when needed.

No one person influenced me. I have learned a lot by observing how others do things—both negatively and positively. I try to assimilate the good aspects of what I observe and try to make sure I don't assimilate the negative.

Several executives said that when facing a stressful situation or when they did not know what to do, they visualized talking to the person—usually calling his name (in all instances where this occurred, the people addressed were men) and asking what he would do in this situation.

Bosses played a significant role in paving the way for the women. Although the women predominantly discussed how their male bosses had helped them, many women had a female boss some time in their career life. The bosses were described as highly respected, intelligent, politically savvy, articulate, and knowledgeable about the system. Many women said they might have made it without these people, but it would have taken longer. These bosses provided the opportunities for the woman to be visible and to be noticed.

> My fourth supervisor strengthened my writing and was my management mentor.

> He gave me more responsibility and did not micro-manage yet provided support and accountability.

> [Boss] indicated that my only experience was as staff to management and that it was a different role to be the decision maker taking the risk for advancing and making decisions. He said he would no longer just take my ideas and accept them as his own; that if I wanted to affect events, I would have to advance my ideas. The very next day, he refused to advance an idea that I gave to him in front of a room full of people. He whispered that if I believed in my concept, I must sell it. So I ventured out and did sell the idea. I learned that it is unsettling to expose oneself to the criticism and risking of ego that advancing one's ideas could provoke. I also learned to organize my thoughts into a succession that would sell my ideas to others.

The women acknowledged that they were responsible for their own career progress but found the advancement was easier with the help of others.

> The primary responsibility for advancement in a career lies with the individual; however, assistance which is offered should be welcomed. Some effort should be spent learning who's who in the organization and assessing who is held in high regard and why. Before making a career decision, there should be some weighing of what a move will do to advance long-range goals. An important consideration is who is the boss; how does this person size up in the organization; will the support of this person be helpful to me in the long run. While an influential executive will make the decision to support or not support a subordinate, it is up to that subordinate to make sure her performance warrants the support.

FINDING THE RIGHT BOSS

There is no one way to select a boss who will provide opportunities and experiences that make a difference in a career, but asking the following basic questions can guide the decision:

- Do you trust the person?
- Can you talk and discuss issues of importance to you, especially about your strengths and weaknesses?
- Is this boss respected in the organizational culture?
- Is the boss known for developing the staff or ruling as a micro-manager?
- What kinds of risks does the boss allow you to take?
- Is she supportive of you even if you may be wrong?
- How much rope does she give you before you realize you are hanging yourself?
- How many mistakes are you allowed?
- What is her philosophy regarding training, self-development, task force assignments, delegation, recognition and work values?
- Does she take sufficient interest in her employees to know what their career objectives are and ask how they see themselves attaining them?
- Do you possess skills, knowledge, or ability that threatens the boss?
- Does the boss believe in the scarcity principle (the more of the pie she gives away, the less there is for her)?
- What kind of power does she possess?
- What kind of boss do you want?

These questions, and others as well, are designed to awaken career thinking and an understanding of the importance of a boss. The bottom line in selecting the best boss is to find a match between what you need and want with what he or she offers.

Role models are important to career progression as well. They are usually hard workers who play fair, show weaknesses and strengths, admit failures and learn from them, strive to be the best but not demand perfection of themselves or of others, have values reflecting their principles, are assertive yet humble, are humorous, have high energy, are knowledgeable, and share information. Most of all, role models know themselves and are comfortable enough with themselves to have confidence in their skills as leaders and followers. Fitting these descriptions as role models are women such as Frances Perkins (popular with many of the women over age 50), Eleanor Roosevelt, Esther Peterson, Elizabeth Dole, and senior women within the organizations of the women in this study. The most popular role model, noted by over 12 percent of the respondents, was Connie Newman, former OPM director. To many, she represented the ultimate leader in public service, and many of the women were trying to emulate her management and leadership principles: fairness, loyalty, candor, orientation toward people, political savvy, intelligence, and knowledge of government.

To incorporate the role model's principles into one's own self-development plan is to learn how to mirror the role model: that is, distinguishing the characteristics that are admired about the person and incorporating these qualities into your own portfolio. Examples of these could be image, confidence, philosophy, public speaking ability, communication skills, values, humor, and interpersonal skills. The more you know about these qualities, the easier it will be to have them be part of your own behavior.

In this study, more men than women were described as role models. Some of the women expressed that they wished there were more women role models. Another study has noted that the dearth of women in power and authority to emulate has been a career obstacle to other women, although none of the SES women believed that a lack of female role models had hindered their careers.[1]

MENTORS

Another key player in this people domain was a mentor. Of these 78 SES career women, 65.4 percent had had a mentor at some time in their careers. A mentor was defined as anyone who helped, advised, or guided the person, looked out for them, made special opportunities for them, or protected them when they took risks. Most of the mentors were older and well tuned to the system. For the most part, they were bosses, husbands, peers, and superiors (two to three levels higher in the hierarchy). They knew the ropes of government, they knew the people in government, and they knew how to work the system. These relationships were usually very informal, and some of the mentors were not aware they were playing this role:

> Person didn't know he was my mentor. I grew in the job. [He] looked out for me and gave me awards. I was a producer.

The sharing of experiences and having access to organizational information as well as the persona of the individual mentor and the opportunities presented by the mentor were significant for the "mentee" in how quickly she learned how government worked. Some women mentioned only one mentor, but many had several mentors at different stages of their careers who had moved them in the right direction and encouraged them to continue forward. The timing also varied, from brief time spans to as much as the entire course of the career.

> There were several men who taught me the ropes along the way. The one that stands out the most didn't teach me much I hadn't already learned, but he encouraged me to go for the top. He was an Army General when I was a GS-11. He encouraged me to come to Washington. We've kept in contact even though he's retired. Whenever I think I can't, I call him.

The importance of mentors was elaborated on in a 1992 report by the U.S. Merit Systems Protection Board (MSPB), *A Question of Equity*, which consolidated the 8,400 survey responses from executive branch employees in grades GS/GM 9–15 and SES and found that women derive more benefits from mentors than men do. This report noted an increasing number of women who are being mentors and indicated that women tend to go to peers for informal information. As more women enter the pipeline, established mentoring programs will be common. The Department of Transportation and the General Services Administration, among other federal departments, have already initiated formal mentoring programs.

Finding a Mentor

In seeking a mentor, each person must begin by deciding what she wants from this relationship: a guide, a supporter, a motivator, a teacher, an adviser, a safety net, a door opener, a mover or shaker, a sharer of knowledge, a leader, a role model, a respected person, a political appointee, a survivor, or a friend. Once these qualities are decided, the search for the people who meet the requirements can begin. Help in the search can come from peers, friends, human resource professionals, a boss, and other associates.

Once the person is identified, the next step is to contact the person and set up an appointment to explain to her that you would like for her to be your mentor and why. After this meeting, you should be able to determine if she is supportive of the idea, has the time and patience to work with you, and is willing to share her knowledge and insights. If the agreement is mutual, the two of you can draw up a plan that will incorporate both mentor and protégé's goals, spelling out time commitments and resources required to make the relationship work for both parties. This relationship can be the beginning of a career turning point, as it was to 65.4 percent of the executive women in this study.

Ending the Mentor Relationship

The mentoring relationship is one of professional and personal growth and demands energies from both parties. Sometimes the mentor relationship needs to be terminated, for a variety of reasons: the protégé outgrows the mentor, one or both parties takes a new job, the mentor exploits the relationship, the expected benefits are not met, or the expectations of one or both parties are too high.

In the research, many women expressed how difficult it was to realize they had outgrown the mentoring relationship. When the woman started to be more independent and have more confidence in herself and her skills, she knew it was time to move forward without her mentor. Confronting the mentor with this information was hard for many of these women, because they felt indebted in some way to the mentor for their assistance. Yet many believed it was the healthy approach for all involved. For two women, the mentor relationship had become stressful because the men had taken romantic interests in them; ending the relationship was difficult. Also, in two separate instances, the women married their mentors.

FAMILY

Another prominent player in the people area was the woman's husband. Husbands were role models, supporters, friends, and mentors. Many of the respondents discussed the support that was required by the husband as she plotted her career. One woman had the distinction of making the front pages: she was the first woman in her city where a husband followed his wife for her career change. Also discussed was the role the husband played in helping to rear the children and run the household. Equally discussed were the trauma and friction that arose when the woman was more successful than her husband, when she competed for the same position, when she had to work late or cancel vacation plans, or when she had to move geographically.

> My former husband resented my career to the point where it became a constant friction between us. Instead of having a support system at home, I had to confront him and grow as a manager in spite of his reactions. I eventually achieved regardless, but it would have been a lot more pleasant had this friction not been present. I believe it contributed significantly to my tenseness during my formative career progression.

Children too contributed to the women's success, both positively and negatively. Some said by having children they were able to empathize more with their employees. Others said their employees sometimes acted as children, and they were able to manage them with more awareness and sensitivity. During different stages in their careers, having children influenced the direction of their careers.

NETWORKS, ASSOCIATIONS, AND FRIENDS

Networks, associations, and friends played a limited part in the career progression of these women. Networking, defined to include all contacts, both short and long term, that offered the women information, access to opportunities, and a sounding board for ideas, was a valuable ingredient in the career advancement of these women. Through networking, they learned about position openings, found out helpful information, had a sounding board, exchanged data on how to do the budget or an operating plan, or were introduced to the right people.

In the 1992 MSPB survey, networking was an important factor to women climbing the ladder in learning about career opportunities.[2] In reporting whether a woman knew if the supervisor, the occupant of the current position, or friends of the organization where she applied had helped her obtain the position, more than 50 percent of the women agreed that this knowledge had made a difference in their career advancement.

In addition to promotions, networking provides an indirect advantage: being part of the web of inclusion, that is, the informal network within an organization. Many people believe that the informal organization is where the major work is accomplished. According to Marilyn Loden in *Workforce America!*

> Inclusion in the informal networking process is empowering and important to career advancement. Information about key decisions, how performance is evaluated, and what lies ahead are often revealed during informal interactions that occur over lunch, dinner, or in social settings. In the absence of current information, it is far more difficult to be confident about the future or to understand the potential impact of organization changes on personal and career goals.[3]

Those who know the system, are given the right information for their work to be visible, and receive the right resources to implement the project are better prepared and will gain recognition that pushes them to the top of the ladder. It is in this informal work-related information and advice that women experience exclusion, especially in a hierarchy composed of the "old boy" networks. Learning to play the networking game was an important lesson for the career executive woman to master and integrate into her career progression. The importance of networking was summed up in this way:

> Networking is important to give advice and invaluable information. Have ideas and can try these ideas on people. [It gives you an opportunity to] bounce ideas off of people.

Several women noted that professional associations (such as the American Bar Association or the American Medical Association) had helped them, protected them, and projected their careers. These associations were very specialized, usually of the specialty field where the woman was known as an expert.

Friends too played a special role; they provided solace, support, and camaraderie. It was almost like escapism for the women to be with friends and to be away from the stress of the workplace. The lack of friends was mentioned as a concern; the progression up the career ladder left less time to be sociable. Several women were making efforts to have time for self and others.

MENTORS TO OTHERS

Many of the SES women were mentors to others. They were more than casually involved, and many looked upon this as one of their main goals. They discussed choosing people to mentor whom they could help and guide through the system of government. They also gave advice to the upcoming managers to have several mentors and have them early in their careers.

I always encourage people that I counsel (and I am a mentor for many) to set goals, five years at a time, concentrate upon them, accomplish them, and then reset them again. I encourage them to obtain as many mentors as possible and utilize them sensitively and selectively.

SUMMARY

All of the people involved in the career progression of the women helped them. For the most part, they were there when they were needed, encouraging and creating an atmosphere for opportunities to pull the women up to the next rung of the ladder.

Rosabeth Moss Kanter, in *Men and Women of the Corporation*, has discussed the importance of alliances, especially in the careers of women. If people do not have "informal political influence, access to resources, outside status, sponsorship, or mobility prospects," she says, they "are rendered powerless in the organization." She defines powerlessness as "the general condition of those people who could not make the kinds of powerful alliances that helped to manage the bureaucracy. People without sponsors, without peer connections, or without promising subordinates remained in the situation of bureaucratic dependency."[4]

Other authors too have pointed to the importance of having a mentor, including Gail Sheehy (*Passages*), Daniel J. Levinson (*The Seasons of a Man's Life*), Michael Zey (*The Mentor Connection*), and Ruth Halcomb (*Women Making It*).[5] A 1982 study of 1,086 top and middle executives, *The Cox Report on the American Corporation*, "strongly suggests that having a mentor can have at least as positive an effect on one's career as having a Masters of Business Administration degree from a prestigious university."[6]

All relationships—mentors, bosses, husbands, children, networks, peers, friends—influenced the career progression of these women. They showed the ropes, taught the system, put them in the trenches, designed the route, gave support and encouragement, created the opportunities, and paved the way. These types of relationships and their effect were vital considerations in determining how, who, and what made the difference in these 78 SES women's career tracks.

NOTES

1. W. Booker, R. Blair, M. F. Van Loo, and K. Roberts, "Are the Expectations of Women Managers Being Met?" *California Management Review* 27 (Spring 1985): 148–157.

2. U.S. Merit Systems Protection Board Report, *A Question of Equity: Women and the Glass Ceiling in the Federal Government* (October 1992), 24–27.

3. Marilyn Loden and Judy B. Rosener, *Workforce America!* (Homewood, IL: Business One Irwin, 1991), 40.

4. Rosabeth Moss Kanter, *Men and Women of the Corporation* (New York: Basic Books, 1977), 186–188.

5. Gail Sheehy, *Passages: Predictable Crises of Adult Life* (New York: E. P. Dutton, 1976); Daniel J. Levinson, *The Seasons of a Man's Life* (New York: Alfred A. Knopf, 1978); Michael Zey, *The Mentor Connection: Strategic Alliances within Corporate Life* (New Brunswick, NJ: Transaction Publishers, 1990); Ruth Halcomb, *Women Making It, Patterns and Profiles of Success* (New York: Atheneum, 1979).

6. Cited by Martin Lasden, "A Mentor Can Be a Millstone," *Computer Decisions*, March 26, 1985, 74–81.

7

Finding the Career

Deciding what career to pursue, planning how to do it, and entering the field were major stepping-stones in determining the women's pathway. The effect of a particular occupation on the executive's career success was also explored. Stages of development were discovered that could be linked with the experiences and lessons that the executive used as she moved up the ladder.

OCCUPATION

According to the government's classification system, these 78 women were in the business of, and classified in, 28 different job series (a classification system to categorize major job tasks, duties, and responsibilities). Each person within the government is associated with a particular series and grade commensurate with the knowledge, skills, and abilities brought to the position. Six job categories represented 82 percent of the senior executive women's job series:

201	(Personnel)	9.0 percent
301	(General Administrative)	43.6 percent
505	(Financial Management)	5.1 percent
601	(Health Sciences)	3.5 percent
905	(General Attorney)	15.4 percent
1301	(Physical Scientist)	5.1 percent

These six job categories are also representative of the total government work force.

A majority of the women had not planned for a particular occupation, although those who had attended college expressed their interests in certain fields by choosing a major. (Whether this degree was used in their occupation was a different matter.) These women majored in 26 different fields of study. The predominant areas were political science (22 percent), business administration (9 percent), psychology (9 percent), and math, English, and sociology (each 4 percent). Education played a large role in helping define what occupation was chosen. A law degree (19.2 percent) was the largest single degree earned by the respondents.

> A law degree has sometimes symbolized the way to get in the door of public service and to have respect. A law degree can sometimes be a passport into the intricacies of public service.

Identifying exactly how they chose their occupation was difficult for the women to articulate: it just happened, it was there, or it evolved. The questionnaire did not ask specifically about choosing an occupation, but in the answers, the women discussed choosing to go into law, medicine, research, personnel, budget, engineering, and social science. Women who had acquired a professional (law, medicine) or doctorate degree were committed to obtaining the credentials required for their field.

> Prior to law school I worked at various jobs. After law degree, it put me into the category of lawyers.

Although many of them related that their chosen career was not their initial choice, it became a focus early. For the women in the General Administrative series, the occupation specialty was set depending on how and where they came into the government—government examinations, a college degree, or an intern program. Many discussed going into "this occupation" because they wanted interesting work or they liked the field (writing, personnel, budget, program management, program officer, adviser, or generalist). For those in the administrative specialist areas, such as personnel, budget, and finance, the women said they were exposed to these fields and found they liked the variety, people, and responsibility offered. Few said they determined to be in that occupation and proceeded by a plan. The following description is typical:

> Started out as a management intern, classical career progressions: classification, employment relations, moved up the supervisory chain, from a little supervisor to a big supervisor, from a manager of a major department to the responsibility of being the "it" with an independent agency. Moved to different agencies to get the experiences required to continue to progress and learn about how the system works.

EDUCATION

Based upon the average age of 46 for these women, they graduated from high school in the early 1960s, a time when women were going to college in increasing numbers and looking at a future that encompassed more than marriage and family. Some went to college to get a teaching degree or to do something in business, some to find a suitable spouse, and some because they sought work opportunities beyond the traditional ones for women (clerical, secretarial, or nursing). Over 94 percent of these women had some college, with 90 percent having a bachelor's degree or above. Very few took the direct route going from high school to Ph.D. without any break for work, but those who did were very career oriented and determined. Only one woman (the youngest respondent) discussed how she had consciously planned what she wanted to do and sought people out to guide her. One of her professors had suggested a turn for her career that might be more lucrative and in line with her interests. She earned a doctorate in a different field than she had planned and was able to get a position using her education.

AGE

Age was another factor in choice of occupation. The women between ages 55 and 66 grew up in a totally different atmosphere regarding women in a world of work. They set the standards in how women were perceived. Many liked this role; others felt it interfered with their lives. The answers from these women reflected an enormous variety of experiences, different levels of responsibility, and a pioneering attitude toward their work. They were loyal and dedicated to their departments, with most of them spending their entire career at a single department. Some said that hard work and perseverance, rather than a particular career, were key to moving up the ladder.

The women between ages 40 and 55 were transitional women, representing a variety of experiences and work situations. Those at the upper end of the continuum associated more with women who had over 25 years of experience in the government. They tended to be open yet cynical about the system of government. They believed hard work and determination were the crucial variables in their lives. The women at the early end of the continuum looked at those above them and those below them for guidance. Many of these women had been viewed as specialists, experts, or the best in the field before they had moved out of the technician or specialty route. For these women, the road was not always straight and easy to follow. This age group contained the women who tried to have it all: marriage, children, and an impressive yet time-consuming career. They bridged traditional roles with nontraditional positions. They showed that a woman could be part of the system, could play the game, and could be competent yet continue to be true to herself as a woman. They had to fight internal battles (guilt over working long hours, conflicts between work and family, etc.)

with themselves and learn what worked for them. Many of them were successful in this quest of "having it all," but many, after entering the SES, realized that
their careers had consumed much of their lives.

In the age range 33 to 40, the women were more in tune with their occupation and field of study. To some degree, they planned their opportunities and
how to use their education to open doors. The women in this age bracket were
more educated, with more law and professional scientist degrees, and most of
them took it for granted that they would be the best in their field. This goal does
not equate with rising to the top ranks of management. For many of them, management and leadership were not in their plans; they just wanted to be the best
in their field.

The experiences and the education of these women, as well as the environment of the world and, in particular, the government, were determining factors
in how well they adjusted their behavior (ethics, philosophies, value systems) to
their chosen occupation. At all of the ages, it was important to have knowledge
of the position, awareness of the environment (including the political context),
familiarity with role responsibilities and behavioral demands, and the ability to
exert power and influence over one's own skills and capabilities. Added to these
to provide a picture of the executive woman at all ages are self-confidence, determination, and hard work.

THE ONLY OR FIRST ONE

In all age groups, 30 percent of the women were or had been the first or only
woman to do that particular job or play that particular role. The occupations
varied for this experience. These "first" women experienced a variety of obstacles, including isolation. When seeking advice or guidance, they usually turned
to colleagues, peers, or superiors. Their determination to succeed was evident,
and they were committed to accomplishing this goal. Proving that women could
do this task was important to them.

CHANGING OCCUPATIONS

The timing of entering the government was only one factor. Another variable
was the department they entered for their first job. Generally, how a department
felt about women in the workplace determined how each woman was employed,
what opportunities were available, and how much support she received. Some
started their government careers in clerical roles, although they had college degrees. Getting the foot in the door was the object of finding a job and then learning how to work themselves out of this role into a technical or professional
specialty. The culture and, to some extent, the environment of an organization
were significant considerations in getting promoted out of the clerical field and
into the technical and professional fields. In all occupations, it was important for
these women to understand the agency's philosophy on rotational assignments,

task forces, education, training, and specialty programs. For example, the ten women who went through the SESCDP believed that if their agency had not been committed to this program, they would not be in the SES; they may never have had the training that was required in order to make it to the top.

Other women came up through the ranks. All of the approaches to changing occupations played a major part in how these women progressed. This movement through various positions not only helped the women choose an occupational field but also built self-confidence.

Over the career span of these women, many have changed positions; some have changed occupations. They moved from personnel to procurement, from logistics to staff, from operations to staff, from accountant to financial officer or budget manager. Others changed agencies to get a wider breadth of their own field, such as moving from practicing tax law to practicing environmental law. These women were aware of the need to take advantage of opportunities and to be flexible and focused, especially when they moved laterally within their own organization. Some, due to life experiences (divorce, children, politics, organizational mistakes, or tragedy), were forced to change occupations. For many, they learned from their past experiences and were able to learn and restart—in some cases, finding better positions and a faster career ladder than the previous job had offered.

Except for law, science, and medicine, very few of the occupations selected by the women were planned in a systematic way. Additionally, for the most part, a particular occupation was not the major crux of why the executive was successful. The women believed they achieved their successful careers by luck, timing, good education or training, hard work, long hours, and support from others.

More than 43.6 percent of these women were in administrative-type occupations, compared to 35 percent of the overall SES population. The government's classification system varies by department. Also, some employees, when they reach the SES, leave their specialty series and are given a generalist rating. For example, several lawyers experienced this, as did researchers, personnel officers, and human resources directors.

ADULT DEVELOPMENTAL STAGES

These women dispelled the theory of developmental stages of careers that follow predictable stages associated with a particular age. These women did not follow any set developmental research models (such as those of Erikson, Cross, Havinghurst, or Levinson). They were all individuals who lived their lives not in 15-year increments with set predictions of what would happen to them at various ages, but rather developed their careers by various means. Because of the fluidity of the job market, changing demographics, the shortage of skilled labor, and changing life-styles, these models do not fit the majority of women in this study. Betsy Jaffe, in *Altered Ambitions*, found that early adult development research is not applicable to working women. In fact, she says, these models do not "fit the latest generation of men [either] whose priorities and career patterns are shifting too."[1]

If these women were forced into a pattern, it would have to follow a loose network of cluster events. The general stages of these 78 SES career women as defined by the data were:

Stage 1   Learns about the job itself.

Stage 2   Gains more confidence and becomes more technical.

Stage 3   Learns about the system; apprenticeship.

Stage 4   Supervises others; more responsibility.

Stage 5   Staff position.

Stage 6   Manager.

Stage 7   Executive.

Stage 8   Mentor.

Stage 9   Acceptance of one's achievements (retirement).

These nine stages represent a new adult development model for career women. Although this model emerged from this study of government women, it could be broadly applied to non-government women as well. Unlike many other adult development models, this does not start or finish at a certain time. Nor is it linear; it can go up and down and horizontally as the woman obtains more experiences and a wider depth of knowledge. In each stage, continuing education, obtaining credentials, or being a self-directed learner is integrated and depends on the needs and strengths of the individual and the job. In addition to the professional route described in stages 1 through 9, these executive women were always looking for learning opportunities: they changed jobs, experienced career setbacks or hardships, rethought their careers, changed direction, and balanced personal and professional life.

From this general progression and the incorporation of the learning opportunities, there were no set patterns associated with developmental stages defined by Erikson, Havinghurst, Cross, or Levinson that applied to the executive women. If we broadly define the stages and take into account the movement back and forth (called the learning opportunities between and during stages), Erikson's model is the most closely attuned to these 78 SES career women:[2]

Age 20–40   Early Adulthood (Intimacy versus Isolation).

Age 40–65   Middle Adulthood (Generativity versus Stagnation).

Age 65+   Later Adulthood (Integrity versus Despair).

Patricia Cross's model, which includes psychological and behavioral aspects, was also helpful in exploring the various stages of women in both professional life and roles outside the work environment.[3]

The largest variable associated with the stage the woman was experiencing in her professional life depended on her role as a mother and/or spouse. Having and caring for children, having a relationship, and starting a family were considerations that played a major role in career progression. One woman purposely stayed in her job as a deputy because it allowed her flexibility to have more time with her children. Another left an important position in private industry to work for the government, because it would give her more time to have a baby. Others did not accept positions or opportunities that would have elevated them to positions with more status or higher salaries than their husbands. Until the world of work interfaces with a structure to accommodate the needs of families, it may be difficult to eliminate this stage of a woman's career life.

Other stages affecting career progression are a rethinking of the role of work and its integration with a more relaxed way of living. This stage is not accounted for in the other adult development models because it is a relatively new phenomenon—people living longer and taking earlier retirement. Now people are trying to obtain a better balance between living and working. This has started to change the patterns of how a person develops, chooses a career, works, retires, or begins another career (volunteer or paid). Age was not a boundary to these 78 women.

SUMMARY

Two major implications can be drawn from this knowledge about occupations and developmental stages. First, it leads to the creation of a new and flexible adult developmental model for career women. The realization that there are no set times to be at stage 1, or to go through a particular incident, or to be at a certain point in a career can free up women to explore their own interests at a timetable of their own making. Second, knowing the major occupations these 78 SES women held may be important to those planning careers. Three major occupations—general administrative, law, and personnel—of the six job categories composed 68 percent of all jobs of the 78 SES women. Each occupation requires certain qualifications before moving to the next level, and each possesses the competencies that OPM's Qualification Review Board has classified as an SES position. This information can be important to plotting a course of action early in a career. Of course, other variables are relevant too: the person's strengths, weakness, abilities, attitude, interest, and qualifications. Another point to consider concerns the occupations that will be required to run the government in the year 2000 and beyond. Knowing which occupations are growing and which ones are waning can increase the chances of being qualified for a contemporary occupation. It may not matter to career progression which occupation is chosen initially; but it does seem to matter what one does in this occupation.

General knowledge of progression through a career is helpful in designing action plans and reinforces the concept that it is something that everyone goes through. Getting started early is valuable in obtaining early work experience and confidence, a concept reflected in the advice offered by the women to up-and-coming executives: plan your career, find out as early as possible what you want to be or do, and pursue these goals. The earlier competencies are acquired, the sooner self-confidence and credibility can be achieved and personal and professional life goals integrated.

These 78 SES career women believed that an executive will be successful if her behavior, her education, her environment, her sense of values, and her capabilities match with each other and are in line with the organization. Occupation is not a consideration; it is merely the vehicle to show what one can do.

NOTES

1. Betsy Jaffe, *Altered Ambitions: What's Next in Your Life?* (New York: Donald I. Fine, 1991), 13.

2. Erik Erikson, *Childhood and Society* (New York: Norton, 1950).

3. K. Patricia Cross, *Adults as Learners: Increasing Participation and Facilitating Learning* (San Francisco: Jossey-Bass, 1981).

8

The Woman as a Leader

"You are now a member of the Club" was the feeling of one executive when she entered the SES.

This chapter examines the transition to the SES cadre, the jobs these women hold now, their leadership characteristics, and the environment and culture of their organizations. It also discusses how they see themselves and their success—their view from the top. Entering the SES was the pinnacle of most of these women's careers. This journey was called many things—evolving, "oozed into it," an arduous journey, smooth sailing, hard work, and luck (the right place at the right time).

TRANSITION AND ENTRY TO THE SES

The transition from the general manager (GM) level to the SES level or from private sector to the SES position was not easy and not an overnight process. One executive summed it up for many:

> There is no magic track! There are certain tickets to punch—do current job well, have ability, luck, right place and right time.

Others voiced an old cliché that "hard work paid off," but many concurred that "hard work takes you only up to a point." It was this "point" and how they successfully integrated knowledge, personality, and abilities with knowing the right people and having someone who was willing to take an interest in them that made the difference.

Very few of the women had planned a career in government, and few had made conscious decisions to be in the SES, as this woman noted:

I never had a next-week plan. My career just happened.

Those who came up through the ranks thought that the top for them was unattainable, so their main goals were to do the best job possible and to learn as much as they could. Those who came through a professional status—science, research, medicine, or law—considered their specialty area more important than being a top administrator. To be prominent in their field and to be recognized as an expert and well known for their specialty represented getting to the top to them.

The few women who did plan their careers were the youngest of the population. Throughout college they had planned the coursework that coincided with both their interests and what was needed in the work world; they had mentors and were well connected.

Several women described and were proud of the fact that they had never applied for a job (husbands or friends found them jobs) or every job they applied for, they got (they applied only for positions that they wanted, had researched, and knew they would get). These types of experiences stood out for the executive women. They were grateful for the interventions of others into their lives; some of the others "actually forced" the women to apply for their first SES position. Another experience was going from a GM-15 position to the SES position—the people involved, the process to be learned, the strategies employed, and timing of the events.

I was selected for my first SES position. The paperwork had gone to OPM for their approval. The person who selected me left, and I had to wait until [his replacement] came for the paperwork to be processed. I was doing two jobs for two-thirds of the pay. [I had] an intervention for me to OPM by a political appointee; he helped me get into the SES.

The conversion into the SES was not easy for most of the women. It was time consuming; many had been passed over for other SES positions they thought they should have received; they did the job without the extra pay; or the jobs were not there. A woman who had gone through SESCDP was considered eligible for an SES position without going through the Qualifications Review Board again. For some, their eligibility ran out, and they had to recompete. One woman was converted on the very day her eligibility was to expire. Of the ten women who had completed the SESCDP program, several believed that without this training, they probably would not have been considered for SES positions within their agencies.

No matter how prepared they were, the jump for many from a GM-15 position to the SES position was not an easy transition. Of the 78 women there were two exceptions, women who had gone from a GS-14 to SES because they were highly knowledgeable about their fields and acquainted with the head of the agency. The women who came directly from the private sector to government held extraordinary credentials. They were experts, possessed unique skills and credentials, and were well-known throughout the world.

THE SES CAREER WOMAN: A PROFILE

Each of the 78 SES career women held a top-level SES position, ranging in level from ES-1 to ES-6 with the average level of 3.5. These jobs were very influential within their organizations, and they were perceived to be role models. Each wanted to participate in helping others make the transition into the senior ranks.

Throughout the nation, "the average woman executive is forty-six years old," says University of Southern California researcher Marion Wood.[1] The 78 women who participated in this study fit this pattern, with an average age of 45.8 years, and an age range of 33 to 66. In industry, the executive woman, according to CCL studies, is younger, with an average age of 41 years and a range of 30 to 60. The 1988 *Government Executive* survey of SES women showed that 60 percent of the respondents were married; no information was given regarding children.[2] In this study, 69.2 percent of the SES women were married, a figure that is a little lower than the Fortune 100 executive women (CCL study), 74 percent of whom were married. Both the SES women and the private-sector studies indicated 48.7 percent had children. A comparison of these 78 SES career women with the total SES population (career and noncareer) shows that the SES career women are 4.3 years younger, have been in federal service 1.9 years fewer than the average SES member, have been in SES ranks 1.8 years longer, and the SES median level is 4 compared to the 78 SES career women at the 3 to 4 level.

The SES women had worked in the federal service an average of 19.7 years, with a range from 1 to 40 years of service. They were in the SES an average of 5.2 years, with a range of three months to many who had been there since the Civil Service Reform Act (CSRA) and were in a super grade before the transition to SES. Some of the women entered at the SES level, but a majority came up through the various grade levels. Most of those rising through the lower grades spent some time at the GM-14 and -15 levels. The average years in those grades for the respondents were 3.8 years as a GM-15 and 2.6 years at the GM-14 level. Several also entered at the GS 1–4 level and started as a clerk or clerk typist. The education level of the respondents also had a wide range, from high school diploma through doctorates and professional (law and medical) degrees. The SES career woman is well educated. Over 94 percent have some college—from two or three college courses to two or three different degrees, ending at the doctorate or professional level: 39.7 percent hold doctorates or professional degrees (19.23 with law degrees), 28.2 percent have master's degrees, and 21.8 percent have bachelor's degrees. Additionally, 41 percent gained further training at the FEI. (See Table 8.1 for a complete profile.)

The executive jobs comprise a wide breadth of executive-level positions and rank within the system and have a wide scope and broad responsibilities and missions. As would be expected, the respondents' positions and experiences ranged from staff to line; indeed, every respondent had worked in some type of line or staff function. All were supervisors at one time or another in their careers, although some experienced their first supervisory position when they entered the SES position.

The 33 different government agencies in which they worked vary in mission, size, and funding. Each of the respondents held an important position within these agencies that influenced the mission of that organization, made decisions that affected the public, and/or created systems that contributed to the mission, research, or impact of government on the private sector. The size of their resources varied from a few subordinates to those who controlled over fifteen hundred employees in an agency. Some had billion-dollar budgets; some had no funds to carry out and perform their jobs. Some were in policy positions that decided the fate of millions of people in the country. Some worked on legislation that changed people's lives; some were the power behind the throne; others held positions that were creating new directions within research organizations; some made medical life-and-death decisions; and others determined how government operated on a day-to-day basis. All performed important functions that demanded bright, qualified people.

Some of the positions held by the SES women were impressive: some were very visible; some were low profile; some were operational; some were staff. All were important to the government's success in providing public service. The women worked in a variety of professions, with the most frequently listed being accountant, budget officer, personnel officer, human resources director, finan-

Table 8.1
Profile of the 78 SES Career Women

SES level (average)	3.5
Federal service	19.7 years
In SES	5.2 years
At GM-15 level	3.8 years
At GM-14 level	2.6 years
Education	
Bachelor's	21.8 percent
Master's	28.2 percent
Doctorate/Professional	39.7 percent
FEI	41.0 percent
Age	45.8 years old
Married	69.2 percent
Children	48.7 percent

cial analyst, attorney, writer, researcher, scientist, medical doctor, economist, and expert specialist. The titles varied: associate director, deputy director, director, administrator, chief counsel, personnel officer, financial and budget officer, special assistant, assistant commissioner, legal adviser, assistant to, and chief.

The personal characteristics of the women also varied. None had an outstanding characteristic (exceptional physical appearance, personality, or mannerism) that would have called attention to her. Everyone interviewed was impeccably dressed, with the majority in tailored suits and a few wearing expensive, tailored dresses. Several women discussed the importance of being visible and indicated that they used their appearance as a means to be remembered. The height of the person did not seem to have any bearing in their career progression; they ranged from 5 feet to 6 feet. Most of the women were within the ranges of weight for their height. Some said that they were "fatter" than they used to be, but none would be classified as plump or overweight. In fact, many took pride in discussing their exercise regimen and their concentration on maintaining their weight. One executive had a large sign across her wall for reinforcement, EXERCISE AT 11:30. Each person interviewed discussed the energy required to keep the pace that was demanded. Many stated that their positions required them to work 10- to 14-hour days, including taking work home or working on weekends.

The women often used their physical surroundings to display their personality. The offices of the SES women were usually located on the top floors or on the executive level of the organization. Some offices were large and expansive; others were small with partitions, not meeting the General Services Administration's executive space square footage allotments. Some were equipped with expansive, traditional executive wooden furniture, complete with sofas, overstuffed chairs, conference tables, and reading chairs; others were sparsely furnished—desk, chair, and bookcase. Some had antique furnishings; others had contemporary furnishings. Some designed their offices to incorporate their families and outside lives. Some offices were stark. Except for a few "messy" yet organized offices, the majority of the offices were neat and some almost pristine. Many women tried to make their offices conducive to work by having everything at their fingertips. Most offices were equipped with a computer connected to an electronic information system. Some loved the flexibility the computer afforded them by having access to information; others used it only out of necessity.

One executive realized that she spent more time at work than she did at home, so she had arranged her office like a living room, turning her desk to the wall and allowing room for a sitting area with couch, chairs, end and coffee tables, a television, family pictures, and various collections. She hoped this arrangement would encourage her employees to drop in and discuss matters with her. This arrangement played a large role in how she interacted with her staff. All in all, the executive women had made their surroundings as pleasant and comfortable as possible.

Of the 27 agencies cited by OPM with 50 or more SES members, this research population represented all but 3 of the agencies. A total of 33 agencies were represented in the research. The women were located in Washington, D.C. (87 percent) and in the field (13 percent). The demographic breakdown was 72 white, 5 black, and 1 Hispanic. With this breadth of coverage of women participating from the major agencies and the mixture of occupations, age, education, federal service and other indicators discussed above, this group of 78 SES career women represented the SES career women population.

In the careers of these 78 SES women, the differences and similarities were reflected in their actual work, environment, lessons, experiences, and performance as leaders in government. Many women felt that entering the SES was just the beginning. One woman stated:

> The movement to SES was a key change. Everything you have learned comes into being. You are responsible for strategies. You see things from a strategic viewpoint. You must motivate people to work and deliver the products. You recognize the interplay internally and externally of your own organization.

This woman was experiencing some of the executive functions discussed by Chester Barnard in his 1968 book, *The Functions of the Executive*.[3] These executives were leaders and felt personally accountable for their organization's destiny; they communicated the organization's goals and created a climate for people to work and share information, elicited involvement and participation from their staff, and rewarded them accordingly. Contemporary terms for these functions are *total quality management, empowerment*, and *vision*.

Many of the women felt successful in their jobs; others felt as if they were treading water. To be successful in their SES jobs was an ongoing process. Many worked long hours, including evenings and weekends. Several had little time for relaxation. Time was a precious commodity; it went by too fast, and there never seemed to be enough of it. Although the job as a leader was time-consuming, the rewards were worth it.

CHARACTERISTICS

In discussing what they thought made them successful or when they realized they were going to be successful, the women discussed events where their characteristics or special traits stood out. For those interviewed, a specific question was asked: What characteristics would they use to describe themselves? Sixty-one of the respondents identified 250 different characteristics. Fifty of these characteristics were cited as important by 5 percent of the population. Twenty-three characteristics received a ranking of 10 percent or more. The top ten characteristics listed are:

Intelligent, smart, bright	39 percent
People oriented	33 percent
Hard working	25 percent
Honest, ethical, integrity	23 percent
Energetic, high energy/stamina	20 percent
Loyal	20 percent
Well organized	16 percent
Fair	15 percent
Impatient	15 percent
Caring	15 percent

One or more of the top three characteristics was intermingled into at least one event or lessons learned by these women. The top characteristic, intelligent, is not a surprise; many of the women made special efforts to be knowledgeable in their fields and learn the system of government. The second characteristic, people oriented, was also to be expected because of so many of the events discussed—managing people, learning from others, and working with people. Hard working goes with the executive territory; many of these women described their typical workday as exceeding ten hours. When the women expounded on their own characteristics, many of them believed these top three would almost be mandatory for successful entry into the SES.

ON THE JOB

Jobs, tasks, levels of subordinates, the mission, staffs, budgets, and activities varied, but what did not vary was the scope of the position and the responsibility of the executive to do a quality job. Over and over again, this theme emerged; each woman was determined and committed to her job and to public service. Each wanted to make a difference in how government was run and how it could be improved.

The following question was posed: "Are you in a situation from which you expect to learn something new and if so, please describe." The answers reflected that 67 women felt they were learning in their jobs; 8 said they were comfortable in their jobs and were satisfied handling the normal complex challenges of government; and 3 did not answer the question. In most instances, the executives described their present job and the work that was currently being accomplished. Of the 67 "yes" answers, 20 women were in new jobs, new organizations, new functions, or doing new projects; 5 women had new bosses or new agency heads. More than 37 percent of the women occupied jobs that were in some ways new to them. Many of them believed change and movement were part of the culture of government. Within this question, the women discussed the major components of their jobs: culture, environment, people, and product (content).

Communication

Communication crosses all four categories of culture, environment, people, and product. The women discussed the importance of communication and how they kept in touch with their staff. Managing by walking around was a popular way to stay in touch. They described changing the environment of an organization and solving some problems by creating a climate in which everyone talks and shares information.

> Initiated an awards program. Day of ceremony, for the first time people brought families. People were recognized in local newspaper. I put in new suggestion boxes (I had the only key). All suggestions have value. Every two weeks printed suggestions. I make sure people get to me directly. I recognize people are the most important product the organization has and try to let my employees know this every day.

> One year ago, I faced a demoralized staff and proceeded with the assistance of two skilled management development consultants to work with each individual and the group as a whole to turn the organization into a more productive and satisfied part of the total [agency]. As we stand on the brink of a major re-alignment in structure, I already see a group pulling together and far less resistant to an ever-increasing workload. I continue to learn from this process and am challenged to follow through on more of the staff's own recommendations for change in the context, of course, of the [agency's] evolving new directions. Despite budgetary constraints, it is an exciting time for innovative thinking not only about staff development but also about the future complexion of research funding in the U.S. and abroad.

People

Co-workers higher than the executive and those whom they related to as a boss or peer occupied a large part of the executive's day. For most of the women, their workday was almost consumed by people at meetings, on the telephone, or counseling or guiding the staff. What and how they saw themselves determined to a large extent how successful they felt in performing their jobs.

> I have again moved up the ladder. Have to continually assess the values of the system and the styles of the people you work with to get most out of the job—advance goals of the organization; find the right people for jobs; allow junior people to grow if they are capable and willing.

> My organization is being moved into another area of the agency. The individual in charge is very bright and hard-working but is also abrupt and often abrasive to his staff. He also has a reputation as a micro manager.

This combination will be difficult for me to deal with. I'm sure if I survive I will learn something—at a minimum what not to do; hopefully I will also pick up some positive pointers.

I walk around and know my people. I feel I must walk around and be seen.

I have a new job—in two years, for the second time I have succeeded my boss—I have my old job to oversee plus the budget—new areas to me.

Environment

These women came from 33 different government agencies: large, medium, and small; defense and nondefense; with old conservative or young and new missions; scientific and research oriented, or mostly administrative program oriented; and small to large budgets. All of these agencies nevertheless shared two characteristics: they had at least one political appointee and they served the public in some way.

The environmental issues discussed (such as physical surroundings, institutional processes and relationships, etc.) ran the gamut from their differences to their similarities. The most frequently discussed environmental issue was the impact of the political system.

To survive in the government, one must not only know the political system but its interaction with the environment of the organization and outside groups such as Congress, interest groups, unions, and the press.

Learning to steer a steady course during economic constraints and an increasing demand for output. We must collect information to craft answers. Any response will be debated by scientists, Congress, and the press.

Can't be a wild-eyed idealist and survive. There is a bottom line budget. What I think about it is not printable.

Like small agency environments because you are able to see immediate reactions.

Like most aspects of my present job, there is no perfect work environment.

You must operate within the sensitivity of the environment you work in.

Learning to stay alive in the political environment and turning it to your advantage.

My management team and I are working together to plan for the future of my organization. We envision major changes in size, composition and structure. The union will have a keen interest in what we will be doing. We've done this one before, but I don't think the situation can be presumed to be similar. Time has made changes.

Culture

"Culture" has many meanings, but the one that was applied by these women fell in line with the definition by Edgar H. Schein in *Organizational Culture and Leadership*:

> Culture: a pattern of basic assumptions—invented, discovered, or developed by a given group as it learns to cope with its problems of external adaptation and internal integration—that has worked well enough to be considered valid and, therefore, to be taught to new members as the correct way to perceive, think, and feel in relation to those problems.[4]

The government has its own culture; its uniqueness is further defined at the organizational level. For the most part, the women discussed the culture of their organizations as bureaucratic, hierarchical, and, at the top, mostly white and male.

> The culture of the organization is old and reserved, composed of white males.

> The higher-ups believed that technical experience was required to do certain jobs. If you don't have this, no matter how good you are, you will not be promoted into the position. Technical discrimination.

> I have all men reporting to me. It has changed how I operate. I have adapted to their culture, not theirs to mine. Because I have three brothers I was raised on sporting events; it has helped me be successful and to understand how boys operate.

> Organization has gone from 4 to 5 tight team members to expansion of over 30 people. Original sense of closeness is gone. I am trying to learn how to get the team spirit back into the group.

Job Content

The process of the job and the result delivered by it were the responsibility of the executive. The goal of the executive was to create the atmosphere whereby her staff would be empowered to perform their functions and to get maximum participation from everyone. The women felt that how they acted sometimes made all the difference and created a tone for the rest of the staff. The woman who turned her desk to the wall and made her office seem more like a living

room removed the barriers of communication and made herself more approachable. She noted that her employees had become more productive and
more relaxed. To get the product delivered efficiently and on time, executives
were not detached from the work; they were involved and knew what their staff
were doing and why.

> I supervise 50 people, and at the same time I am responsible for pulling a
> major engineering study together involving many scientific researchers
> both in the U.S. and foreign countries.

> A few parts of my job include supervision, dealing with internal and exter-
> nal organizations, contracting with agencies, exposure to Congress, work
> with people and give them a sense of how they fit together with the agen-
> cy's mission, and the budget process and resources.

> I presently occupy two jobs and have done this for the past one and one
> half years. It's like having a front office (staff) function and at the same
> time can represent a new function and run a division of 30 people from
> hiring, developing, training, to procuring resources to do the job, to as-
> signing projects, tasks and deadlines, to implementing the program.

> My section has the luxury of getting involved in international environ-
> mental issues.

These five ingredients—communication, people, culture, environment, and
job content—are the major conditions and processes in which the executive operates. Her view at the top is influenced by how she integrates these elements
into her professional career.

THE VIEW FROM THE TOP

Getting into SES was the highlight of many of the executives' careers. The
transitional phase was enlightening to most of the executives. When they entered "the Club," many felt unprepared for such responsibility, but most,
through intelligence, interpersonal skills, and hard work, were able to make
their stay in the SES rewarding and meaningful. Their experiences were varied
in content and scope. This was the height of leadership: an opportunity to lead
and create a vision for the organization and see it emerge as a reality.

The view from the top varied depending on how they had made it there.
Some liked the view and being in charge; others felt the top was too demanding
and consumed their lives; still others said they enjoyed the top, and it was worth
the sacrifices that they had to endure; some wanted out. The view also varied
with the content of the job, the organization's culture and environment, the political arena, the adequacy of resources, the budget, new technology, and the relationships among and between superiors, subordinates, and peers. The only

constant given about the view from the top was that each woman responded that she was glad she had made it.

NOTES

1. Quoted in Ann M. Morrison, Randall P. White, Ellen Van Velsor, and CCL, *Breaking the Glass Ceiling* (Reading, MA: Addison-Wesley, 1987), 10.

2. Bobbi Nodell, "Women in Government," *Government Executive* 20, no. 8 (August 1988): 10–20, 57.

3. Chester Barnard, *The Functions of the Executive* (Cambridge: Harvard University Press, 1968).

4. Edgar H. Schein, *Organizational Culture and Leadership* (San Francisco: Jossey-Bass, 1987), 9.

9

Balance and Barriers

To maximize joy, we must minimize our efforts.
Tom Crum, *The Magic of Conflict*

The 78 SES career women have arrived; they have become members of the most prestigious club in government. What barriers did they overcome to make it? What more could they want? Where will they go from here? What is next for them, not only in their careers but in the rest of their lives? Will their future plans affect the government? The answers to these questions are complex. They represented lives—not just one, but many—both personally and professionally. Much thought, time, and consideration was put into this process to determine what was next for them.

THE FUTURE

Projecting their future was easy for some; for others, it was the first time that they had reflected on the process of making it to the top. Through all of this introspection, similar patterns emerged:

Balance life and work (personal goals)	20.2 percent
Present job (new, learning, exciting)	19.2 percent
Reassessment and don't know	17.8 percent
Specific goals	14.2 percent
Find another SES job	7.6 percent
Retirement	5.1 percent

Management skills	3.8 percent
Leave government for private sector	3.8 percent
Unknown	7.6 percent

Balancing Life and Work

The balancing act of life and work, personal goals, and reassessment of their lives were major factors in their lives at this stage of their careers. Women play many roles professionally and personally. Trudi Ferguson and Joan Dunphy, authors of *Answers to the Mommy Track: How Wives and Mothers in Business Reach the Top and Balance Their Lives*, sum up some of the feelings of executive women:

> The notion that women have to make a choice between work and family or that institutions are not responsible for redefining success to include women who decide to have children or that there is something immutable about organization life which requires women to choose between work and family is insidious and distressing.[1]

For most of these 78 SES women, this struggle between the demands of work and family was a reality. Most now felt comfortable enough that they could stop trying to be the "best" and look at what they personally wanted to do; they were ready to start balancing their life with their work. Two major personal goals were discussed: time with children and time for self.

During different career stages, having children influenced the direction of the women's careers. Many of the women with children wanted to restructure their jobs and spend more time with their children. All of the women who had children noted the time requirements placed upon them and sometimes feeling guilty by not being more available to their children. They felt guilty and stressed when work took precedence, and they had to stay late, cancel vacation plans, or miss the mother/daughter banquet. Having better than adequate child care—a reliable family member, a nanny, a live-in housekeeper, or a day care facility—made a difference in how they coped with the stresses of balancing home and work. Many women discussed the "super mom" syndrome; one said she believed in the "mommy track" (whereby she took herself out of the fast career track to be a mother and later, after children were in school, returned to her career); and others said they lived with doing the best that they could.

One woman, whose position of power was instrumental in many of the conflict issues within international circles, was in the process of stepping down from her SES position to stay home, at least part time, to take care of her two small children. She had tried to work out other arrangements, but to no avail; because of her expertise, she was always on call and could be sent overseas with a few hours' notice. She was torn between her responsibility to her children and to her position, which she had worked so hard to achieve. She felt confident that she would be able to return to her specialty area but probably not at the same level.

Several women chose not to have children; they wanted a career and knew that they would not be able to handle both career and family. One woman believed she had sacrificed too much for her career; she realized too late that she did want children.

In addition to the stress for those who had children, many of the women were care-givers of an elderly parent. They felt trapped in the middle between children and parents and experienced stress and guilt when they were not there when needed.

The second personal goal was taking more time for themselves, a decision usually prompted by stressful workloads. Many of these women spent 10 to 14 hours a day at work, and when they arrived home, they were exhausted. Taking care of themselves was, for some, the best priority to begin balancing their lives. The women felt the most confident when they realized they had achieved career goals and now could take care of self; they could relax. They would not give themselves any slack or perform any less efficiently, but they would give themselves permission not to take things so seriously. They planned time to be by themselves—to exercise, take long baths, go for walks with their spouse or significant other, go to the theater or to a movie, or read a "not for work" book.

Some women believed they were balancing their lives and work by integrating both parts of their lives. One woman said she was going to try to stop being "super mom" at both work and home.

I am trying to work less hard and build more leisure time into my life. Am trying to reorganize my present time—to lighten my own load and to give others a chance to demonstrate their talents.

Several women discussed seeking more fulfillment, making life special and happy, and living more each day.

Present Job

For many of the executives staying in their present jobs represented an opportunity for them to make a difference in government, learn the job better, see projects to fruition, or try different projects. Many of these executives were in a learning mode; they had just entered this position through a promotion, transfer, or reorganization, or they had just received a new boss or one was forthcoming. In all of these events, the present job offered many learning opportunities and challenges for the women.

Stay in present job for a while. I really like it; travel is great, and it is exciting.

I want to make changes in the present system and also develop younger managers.

I am committing myself to certain objectives for the next three years which I want to accomplish before I retire. It is a large agenda, but I want to continue to stretch myself and my staff to achieve even higher goals.

In immediate future (as first person to manage this organization) would like to see things come to fruition. Dynamic 5 years ahead.

Reassessment and Don't Know

The "reassessment" and "don't know" categories were similar; the women were trying to determine what they wanted out of life and out of their careers. Those in the reassessment category were in an advanced stage of those who did not know what they wanted to do.

I need to reassess what I really want to do with my life and act on it. Just because you're good at something doesn't mean it's "right" for you.

I need to remain flexible and to do a better job of keeping an eye out for future opportunities. I recognize that in my position I am vulnerable whenever there is a change in leadership in our agency that the new boss will want to pick his or her own person. To date, in my career I have never faced a situation where I wasn't wanted or had to leave.

I need to do some career planning. I have never done career planning. So far, I have been lucky to be invited to other jobs.

I don't know what I want to do. I can't go any higher, because I am in the wrong political party. I get calls from law firms, but they sound so boring in light of what I am doing in the government.

Specific Goals

More than 14 percent of the women related specific goals that they would like to have as part of their futures. In many of these new careers, leaving the government would be required. Three of the respondents wanted to leave the role of administrator or manager and return to their first love, scientific endeavor. In some cases, these were secret dream jobs; others were taking steps to make the job change occur. No time frames were given for these specific goals to be achieved.

I would like to be a dean of a school. As I mature, I want to sit on foundations and do some fund raising. I see myself as a big-picture mover.

Requesting an academic year off to teach in a public administration setting to see different perspectives.

Would like to run an exchange program. Would like to be an advocator for the government.

Up (Find Another SES Job), Over (Leave Government for Private Sector), or Out (Retirement)

Finding another job, leaving government, or retiring made up 16.5 percent of these respondents' future goals. Most of them were not unhappy with their jobs; it was just time to go and move up, over, or out. Most of them had spent much time deliberating about their career success, what they wanted to do, and what they were willing to do. In each area, a major shift of thinking about their jobs and their contributions to government was internalized so that this course of action made sense. Again, no one said this action was on their immediate horizon, although several said that if the opportunity presented itself, they would probably take it.

I may leave government and go into private sector. Maybe do some teaching or consulting. I need to find a better way to handle stress.

I need to find a new SES job. I have been fortunate that opportunities were there when I was interested in career advancement. Now, I need to make sure I have options and opportunities for the future.

Management Skills

Improving their management skills was discussed by 3.8 percent of the respondents. They wanted to be better at their jobs and felt more training or coursework would help them either learn the information or build their self-confidence. Examples of these skills to be learned were to improve "quick response" skills, learn to delegate more, and learn more about project and time management.

I need to continue to improve in communications skills to be sure my expectations are clear and to become more proficient in guiding my management team to develop and present their own solutions to problems, enhancing their feeling of ownership and commitment.

LEARNING

While discussing their futures, the women echoed many of the same concerns about learning on the job, doing new projects and initiatives, getting stale and outdated, lacking training in new technology, and having growth opportunities. They were so occupied and immersed in the daily routine of fighting fires and reacting to crises that there was little time for reflection on what they were doing for themselves and to their families. Burnout and stress were major considerations for leaving the job. The other pattern was to integrate more leisure time and more fun into their work life. In both categories, the women related their need to grow in the job and to have less work with more opportunity for families and themselves.

Attitudes contributed to the success of these women. They were open to learning about their organization, subordinates, peers and colleagues, family, spouse or significant other, children, and themselves. They placed a high value on learning and reeducation on the job. If these learning and growth opportunities were not available, along with the need to balance their lives, they tended to be more dissatisfied with their position.

> Need to move from position; maybe stay maximum one and a half years and then think about next move. I don't want to be jaded with stale experiences and distortions.

To meet all the needs for work, family, and themselves, women must have a positive attitude, enthusiasm, high energy, commitment, and the ability to work hard. Yet they must be balanced physically and mentally, professionally and personally, and, most of all, know themselves. The world of work and family relationships is too complex, varied, and fast paced without recognition that women cannot burn the candle at both ends.

THINKING OF OTHERS

Although these women discussed, for the most part, their own futures with the government, most of them were concerned about others', especially those of women and minorities who are starting their careers or who are already within the pipeline. To them, this is where the government needs to expend some energy and make commitments.

Invisible Barriers

Many took this opportunity to discuss various experiences throughout their careers that had helped or hindered their progression. As they related and reflected on their career progression, their pride was evident. Now that they were trying to simplify their lives and make more time, they wanted to share their thoughts on the invisible barrier within the government. For some, this process made them aware that they had "made it" and wanted to participate in making changes for others. They were entering Erikson's Generativity stage (a time to mentor the next generation of young managers) and, to some, the stage of Integrity (a time to accept one's own achievements and the people who are a part of one's life).

Although no specific question addressed barriers to making it to the top, it was an important issue. More than 82 percent of the SES career women believed there was an invisible barrier. They discussed attitudes of men toward them, being held to higher standards than men, being passed up for promotions and training assignments, contending with sexual harassment, or feeling discriminated against because of their gender. In addition to the invisible barriers, many believed there were very visible barriers that were ingrained into the system.

> In order to get through and reach the top I had to break a lead, opaque ceiling. The barrier is not invisible, because you can see a rash of men and no women. You are not honestly told because you are a woman something didn't happen. It is there. I am used to being the only woman in my environment. Steps are being made. If we stay longer, we could and can see some women come through the steps gradually. We can no longer be better and work harder and make a difference. You need more. I believe affirmative action has made a difference.

There were two major reasons for believing there was a barrier: statistics and attitudes. Some people (27 percent) said statistics showed there was a ceiling. If there were more women in top management, the figures would indicate it, and the ceiling would not be so visible. They also suggested that to counteract these figures, top management and the administration must be committed to make the changes.

> All you have to do is look at the numbers. If we are willing to wait, it might happen. There are many GM-13's and 14's in the pipeline. The best candidates are women coming to government, because men are getting jobs on the outside. Need to keep the pressure on hiring people at the entry level. I have started a breakfast for women at the GM 13–14 level to get them to talk to each other and help them exchange and be exposed to other executives. In large organizations, need to break the stovepipe barrier.

> Just look at the statistics. I don't feel I was ever affected, because I got every job I applied for. There have been improvements. Need to take a longer-term view and make sure we have qualified women at the 15 level. I believe we will see major changes over the next few years. Need to have more role models like Connie Newman. If the Administration would do more, then government will get and respond to this message.

Attitudes

Thirty-one percent of the respondents believed attitudes play a major role in perpetuating the barrier. Many of these attitudes are ingrained in the system and will be difficult to change.

> Some barriers are self-perpetuating. If everyone you deal with is male, and everything you do is male-generated, then you take on these male models and emulate them instead of being yourself. Until this job, I was the only woman in every job I have held since college. Most women as managers are just extensions of men. We learn everything we know from men, which gives a particular slant to everything we do. The system rewards a man's professional pattern. This is still being ingrained into our system; a recent survey by the American Association of University Women of 3,000 school children reflects the different sex roles of boys and girls.

Attitudes were complex, yet they were part of most of the women's systems of knowing and living. They were powerful. Some of the attitudes had major implications in a mixture of settings and cultures:

> It takes more for women to be noticed and considered qualified. Men are considered competent until proven otherwise. Women must prove competence before.

> Men feel women should only go up so high and should not go up high enough to supervise men.

> Women attain power only in certain occupations.

> Many people can't relate well and aren't as comfortable working with women as with men.

> Men are tolerated for mediocrity; women are not tolerated.

> I have always resisted being categorized and stereotyped as a woman.

> Women can't handle certain jobs—military.

> Women are not technically competent.

> Men take courses and say, "I can do it." Women take courses and say, "but I didn't really learn how to do it."

Most of these attitudes reflect things women cannot do or are perceived as unable to do. This type of thinking was also part of the next implication: women limit themselves. Several women discussed the "macho" (authoritarian, male-dominated) image of executive life, and many were not willing to pay the price or make the sacrifice. This again was integrated into trying to make work interface more with living in today's accelerated, changing world.

The women were optimistic that change is in process because of the increase in the number of women in the system and a slow change in attitudes. As the "old guard" (primarily men) retires, more women will be promoted into the SES.

Another discussion was how the older generation's daughters are getting into the pipeline, and there is no better remedy to a problem than when it hits your own backyard. Additionally, the upcoming generation of women has grown up with their mothers' working; there are more role models to follow. As yet, there has been no generation of women that believed it would have to work; women always have had the luxury of choosing either to marry and have children or to work. This is changing; more women are entering the work force for economic reasons. Some are opting to work over marriage, and some have internalized the idea that they will work and are thus planning their careers earlier.

Old Boy Network

The role of the old boy network still exists. But women, too, are starting their own networks and making connections, on a very limited basis. Many of these women said they were not joiners and lacked time for this luxury. Others used their network to find jobs and to learn about other opportunities. Several women mentioned the importance and value of attending the monthly meetings of Executive Women in Government.

The value of the old boy network was not unnoticed by the women. They were jealous of the opportunities and protection that were afforded by such a network.

> The "old boy's network" is alive and kicking. Guy gets into trouble someone will come to his rescue. Woman gets into trouble, she gets it from all angles. Must work a little harder and have more energy to get people to believe she is credible and competent.

The most frequently reported suggestion on how to counteract this barrier was the importance of having top management be committed to change. *Workforce 2000* and *Civil Service 2000* have made all managers and executives aware that the demographics are changing. Agencies are learning more about cultural diversity and how to manage the new work force. Other suggestions for the SES women were to be mentors to upcoming women in their organizations, to provide training and assignments for women in these lower grades, to take initiative to see what agencies require, to do career planning, to create networks, and to support each other.

A majority of the women believed that the changing demographics—the sheer numbers of women coming into the government—would make a difference as the new come in and the old guard goes out, giving room for others to grow. This will not happen overnight and maybe not in the career lifetime of most of these women. One executive cautioned that we need to overcome the tendency to believe that just because there are plenty of women in the system, the numbers will carry it. There are large numbers of women in government employment, but most have not moved into the top ranks. The women believed that barriers exist at all levels, beginning with GS-12 to GM-13 (first supervisory job) to the SES level. A Merit Systems Protection Board survey indicated that the barriers exist even lower, at the GS-9 and GS-11 levels, where women who entered government at the same time as men and have similar education and experience are promoted at a lower rate than men.[2] There are too many unconscious attitudes to be overcome to make more women in the top management positions a reality. A mathematical forecasting model has confirmed that in "25 years, women will still be under-represented at top-management levels."[3] Nevertheless, the SES respondents were optimistic about change and believed the system was improving. With more role models like the senior executive women and an increased general awareness regarding attitudes, commitments to changing the system can make a difference in moving women through the pipeline to the ranks of top management within the public sector.

SUMMARY

The future that the 78 SES career women looked at held many variations. At the same time they were designing their futures, they were being reshaped by the changing demographics, the global world, and legislation, regulation, and court rulings. The many variables associated with work today are causing the role of work to be rethought. In these changing times, women are thinking more about their careers and the price it will cost. The women in this study have reached the pinnacle of government and now are looking at how to balance their life with work. Their high-powered jobs infringe upon their individual lives. Many of the women are happy with their SES positions and enjoy their status. But some, especially the younger respondents, are examining how they feel about work, career, family, and relationships. Some are trying to have it all—careers and an outside life—but stress and burnout are a frequent price. They are also looking at and giving more personal emphasis to leisure time. Others are seeking different kinds of fulfillment through a new SES job, private-sector employment, or retirement. All but a few of the women are reassessing their lives and questioning if they had paid too high a price to get into the SES. The women believed that the image that they can and should do it all needs to be dispelled in order for women to achieve self-esteem and be at peace, not at conflict, with themselves.

Although some agencies have changed their work environments with flextime, flex-place, and flex-hours, these changes usually do not apply to SES positions. The pressures of two-career families, children, and older parents and work pressures of downsizing and early retirements with increased work loads together paint a picture of turbulence for these SES women. How they react to these pressures and stress is part of the reassessment process. Most of the women believed they could and were coping with all of these pressures but they wanted to make life a little easier for those coming through the pipeline. They discussed the barriers to increasing women in top management and made suggestions on how to increase the numbers at the top. Most of them were optimists and believed the system was changing, albeit slowly, and more women would make it into top management.

As women become more comfortable balancing their many roles, they will exhibit a more positive self-image, self-value, self-esteem, and self-respect. This creation of balance will serve as a model for younger women, perhaps easing their route to the top.

NOTES

1. Trudi Ferguson and Joan Dunphy, *Answers to the Mommy Track: How Wives and Mothers in Business Reach the Top and Balance Their Lives* (Far Hills, NJ: New Horizon Press, 1992).

2. U.S. Merit Systems Protection Board Report, *A Question of Equity: Women and the Glass Ceiling in the Federal Government* (October 1992), x.

3. Ibid., 11.

10

100 Steps to the Top

Some are born great, some achieve greatness, and some have greatness thrust upon them.

William Shakespeare

Getting to the top of government is and will continue to be a goal for many public servants. Public service is not just a nine-to-five job but a form of living that enables one to make life easier for others. With this mission in mind, 78 women pioneered the effort to tell their career story in how they moved up the rungs of the ladder that led to the ultimate leadership position within the SES. These women are not only leaders but strategic partners with their subordinates, peers, and superiors who each help create a vision and are able to implement a vision of success for themselves and their organizations.

Although government women were used as the research subjects, the results of the study have wider application. A comparative analysis of 78 private-sector women showed that both public- and private-sector women had similar career progressions and faced many of the same issues. The information provided throughout this chapter and the previous chapters can be broadly applied to any woman (and most men).

IMAGES AS LEADERS

More than ever, women are entering the work world with images of themselves as leaders for tomorrow. With the changing world, specific career pathways of the past may not work, but the fundamental lessons of experience can be the distinguishing step that can make the difference in climbing the next rung of the ladder.

The integration of the 1,356 lessons with the 305 events learned by these women, linked with the knowledge of rapid change and the variety of management philosophies of how to work more productively and efficiently, ensures that women who want to make it can. It will not be easy or quick. It takes hard work, and it takes knowing your internal self and your external coping pressures.

One more element required for the suitcase that is equipped for traveling to greater destinations is to meet the leadership requirements of the position itself. These are very demanding positions that require high energy, intellect, and ambition. Moving up, learning the system, knowing the formal and informal organization, having a mentor as well as other professional networks, and empathy for others are good starts to entry of positions that will lead to the top.

THE SECRET

The secret for future leaders may be the accumulation and possession of a wide range of experiences that provide a diverse perspective for taking risks, managing, leading, and strategizing the future. The government leader of tomorrow must possess the five "F's": flexible, fast, focused, friendly, and fun loving.

Flexible

Over and over the women discussed their flexibility and the importance of being able to change and adapt. In the 1950s, machines were important; in the 1990s and beyond, people are more important and make the difference in the success or failure of an organization. The work environment requires leaders to adapt to multiple requirements: people, laws, regulations, technology, finances, internal and external interest groups, Congress, media, systems, policies, politics, ethics, diverse workforce, and organizational redesigns. Being flexible offers the woman leader the opportunity to redefine the route to the top. She can be the driving force that instills trust and helps chart the new competencies and new skills required of the work force that will be necessary for workers to enter the twenty-first century.

Focused

These women are focused into shifting the negative attitudes and characteristics associated with women to a positively charged culture that captures the strengths of women that are so necessary in making change: cooperation, collaboration, consensus building, and compassion. The myths must be dispelled and the positive nature of women allowed to emerge. New organizational designs and behavioral theories lend support to team building, self-directed teams, group dynamics, partnerships, honesty and integrity, and intuition. All of these areas where women over the centuries have excelled may now, through organizational changes, allow women to practice in a business arena what has come naturally for many.

These trends in management reflect the needs of leaders to be equipped with a high degree of knowledge of interpersonal relationships and a keen understanding of people and their behaviors. This focus on the people aspect of the organization can determine the successful leader and how she operates in a highly diversified and competitive environment. The focus on merging values of a diverse work force and respecting the differences of each culture and the positive characteristics that they provide will be necessary to make the new management theories work in an efficiently run organization. Trust, honesty, and integrity also play a role. People need to feel they can trust their leader; they want someone to be sincere and provide honest feedback. All of these elements will help drive the fear out of the workplace and lead to a productive and caring atmosphere.

Friendly

Leaders must encompass Webster's *Seventh New Collegiate Dictionary* definition of *friendly*: "showing kindly interest and good will; not hostile; inclined to favor; comforting, cheerful." These words symbolize attributes that leaders must possess so that they are able to implement the new management theories of self-directed teams, action learning, and empowerment.

This type of friendliness holds promise of moving a task-centered organization to be a person-centered organization. The workplace will become more human as people feel comfortable and have more self-confidence, which will lead to more productive and efficient organization.

Trust in organizations develops when people value others and share and diffuse power. When open communication is encouraged, morale increases and hostility decreases, with the end result of a better and happier work force. Rensis Likert's study of over five thousand organizations found that high producers were friendly, information sharers, open communicators, good delegators, and trusting, and they created a more efficient operation than managers who did not possess these traits.[1] Trust, open communication, valuing of others, diffusion of power, and sharing of information are wrapped up in the element of friendliness. Women are noted for possessing these attributes naturally, for being interpersonal experts, and for creating consensus-building relationships—all necessary skills desired by a leader of a people-centered organization.

Fast

Fast in this context suggests that efficiency, together with rapid response, ensures accomplishments. These 78 executive women were active participants in all of their positions. They made sure that they learned all that they could and used their vast resources to make the job better and get the task accomplished.

Another definition of *fast*, according to Webster's dictionary, is "daringly uncon-
ventional." Some of the women took risks to accomplish their mission. Others decided to change the system, exchanging traditional ways of working for a somewhat
unorthodox approach to solving problems. By doing this, many became visible and
recognized for their creative methodology and solving the problem quickly and efficiently. This lesson was learned over and over again: sometimes take a risk to be
quick and responsive and do it a different way from the past approaches.

Because of the turbulent changes and fast-moving world, the reinventing of
government, the right sizing of organizations, the developing of business units,
and the diversity of the work force, increasingly there will be a need to be fast
and responsive and more of a sense of doing it right the first time. Women
throughout history have had the ability to juggle many activities at once. As a
home manager, she possessed and performed managerial skills that are used in
the workplace: planning, teaching, guiding, handling conflicts, negotiating, pac-
ing activities, scheduling events, monitoring, disbursing information, meeting
and greeting people, utilizing scarce resources, budgeting, and creating a growing and peaceful environment. In *Megatrends for Women*, Judy B. Rosener says,
"Women leaders try to transform people's self-interest into organizational goals.
. . . Women are likely to thrive in organizations changing or growing fast—
'When change is rampant, everything is up for grabs.' "[2] With these excellent
skills, women have moved into management and leadership with more control
of their changing environment.

Fun Loving

This area is the least noted as an attribute that will make the difference in
how fast one makes it to the top of the ladder. This trait emerged only when the
executive felt at ease with herself and her position in the government. She
wanted to be more fun loving and humorous, but the task and the work involved
with moving up the ladder prevented her from having the time to devote to fun
activities. Yet almost all of the women felt it was important to maintain a sense
of humor and wit, and they worked at trying to take themselves less seriously.
They were learning how to balance work and their outside life and incorporate
fun activities into their home and work environment. This emerged as they created a more congenial work environment and took more interest in other people's activities.

Having more fun in the workplace is almost a contradiction in terms compared to the changes that require more work with fewer resources. This is the
very reason it is so important for the well-being of the individual and the organization to mix work with fun. Stress is a culprit. Fun is one way to alleviate
stress and allow a renewal of spirit.

Learning to balance work and family life is a major issue with today's executive
women. Flex-time, flex-place, and flex-hours, along with adequate health care,
family leave, and child care, provide women the opportunity to incorporate a

more balanced life. These benefits are becoming more available as more women enter the work force. According to John Robinson, director of the Americans' Use of Time Project at the University of Maryland, "Leisure time—not money— is becoming the status symbol of the 1990's."[3] Women, along with the new generation of workers who want more free time than pay, will lead the way to introduce more fun into the workplace and into the lives of so many people.

THE PATH

The path to the top is constantly in flux, but the major foundations of lessons and experiences, as pointed out by the 78 executive women, show that these lessons must be learned and fit to opportunities that come your way. These will then define the specific route for you to follow, and you will know what your organization values. Putting these two ingredients together will map out the route.

Mapping out your particular action play requires you to aspire to and see yourself in the top position. You also must ask: "What have I learned that will move me up the ladder in my career?" You must also know yourself.

Strengths and Weaknesses

Identify your strengths and weaknesses and write them down. Use your strengths to provide yourself visibility and credibility, and continue to work on your weaknesses by recognizing them and incorporating them into your action plan. For example: *Strengths and weaknesses*: "I am good at giving oral presentations and I like people, but I dislike writing and the self-discipline required to accomplish a report." *Action plan*: "Give impromptu speeches; volunteer to give presentations or briefings for top management."

Your successes in your areas of strength will validate you, provide self-confidence, and keep you informed. Assess what needs to be improved: grammar, punctuation, capitalization, content, syntax, style, handwriting and/or computer word processing skills. Once your areas of improvement have been established, make specific "to do" lists with time lines noted by each specific improvement— for example, "I will write my speech out. I will read an English book regarding grammar. I will ask someone to read my writing and provide feedback." Sometimes people discover they are better than they thought. Negative thinking can tear down confidence and erode self-esteem. It is a great morale booster when someone says: "I enjoyed reading your paper, or you write where I can understand what is needed;" or, better yet, "For the first time I know how to do x, y, and z because your instructions were clear."

Getting Out of Your Rut

How can you get out of the rut of coming to work, doing a good job, putting out fires, and learning the job in a way that will allow you to grow and have greater opportunities? To get to the top is an incremental climb, and usually the place to begin is with your present job. Do you feel stuck? Is your job interesting? Are you learning and growing, or are you continually putting out fires that extinguish your own chance for growth? When was the last time you took any training, especially in technology or data automation? When was the last time you volunteered to be on a committee or be part of a task force or just a new project? If the answers to some of these questions are, "I am in a rut; I have stopped learning and growing; I haven't taken on any new assignments or attended a training class within the last year," then you need to ask, "What have I been doing with all my time?" Then ask what you did with the time and how committed you are to make the changes.

Assuming you do want to make the change in your behavior, reread Chapters 4 and 5 to review the lessons and events that appeal to you. Write them down— for example, "I need to learn to have more self-confidence in my skills and talents." "I need to get more training in how to communicate better." "I want to understand more about what executives are like." After you have digested the various lessons that you need to learn, determine where you can learn them: from your boss, training, working on a task force, observing others, or changing jobs.

Another way to get out of the rut is to analyze your job. What do you like about it? What needs does it satisfy for you? Establishing these baseline feelings about your job will help you create opportunities in your own position to fill the gaps within your own experience and training. You can prepare a strategic plan for your job to include how you can help your boss look better; present a new way to be helpful to the organization; plan your involvement in your position and your organization; and show how it benefits both.

There are many lessons to learn and roads that will lead you to your destination. It takes commitment, time, determination, and the five F's—be focused, friendly, fast, flexible, and fun loving.

You may have to open up yourself to look at the potential from within; you will need to believe you can do it, or it will probably not happen. The following 100 Steps to the Top are not inclusive but will help you make it to the top within any organization.

General Ground Rules

1. Be focused in what you really want to be.
2. Be flexible and open to all opportunities.
3. Be friendly to all.
4. Be fast in all your endeavors.
5. Be fun loving and have a sense of humor.
6. Be realistic in your wants.
7. Be prepared to get what you want.

Learning about You

8. Learn to know who you are internally.
9. Learn to like yourself.
10. Learn to assess your strengths and weaknesses.
11. Learn to observe your body language and your nonverbal communications.
12. Learn how your voice sounds.
13. Learn what makes you happy and sad.
14. Learn to take risks.

Relating to Others

15. Ask for feedback from your peers about you as a person.
16. Search for ways to know who you are with others.
17. Observe your own behavior in a group.
18. Discover what or who makes you smile.
19. Explore your reaction to change.
20. Find your place on Maslow's hierarchy of needs.[4]
21. Recognize your talents and how you use them.

Getting Out of the Rut

22. Write your career objective and be as specific as possible. Incorporate the first 21 steps of this list.
23. Write your personal vision statement of you as a person and your philosophy of life.
24. Choose what you want to do.
25. Control your next step.
26. Make the decision to begin today.
27. Recognize your role in making your career happen.
28. Appreciate yourself for deciding to move forward and taking a risk.

Moving Forward

29. Decide on the career you want.
30. List the elements of this career that interest you and those that do not interest you.
31. Ask, "Do my interests correspond to my strengths, and do the dislikes of the job correspond to my weaknesses?"
32. Assess your vulnerability and your risk level.
33. Plan your next move considering the preceding 32 steps.
34. Identify in words what you will do first, then second, third, and so on.
35. Review your career options.

Finding and Applying for Vacancies

36. Find out what is available. A good resource for government is the Federal Research Service (a listing of all vacancies throughout government); buy your own copy and be

the first to see the vacancies. For private sector vacancies look at trade journals and newspapers.

37. Call for the vacancy announcement from the designated personnel office. Apply for vacancies of positions that sound as if the job fits in with your preceding 35 steps.

38. Request as much information as possible regarding the evaluation criteria of the job that you would like to have. Address all mandatory and optional rating criteria. Be specific, and address your accomplishments with honesty and pride.

39. Ensure your Standard Form (SF) 171, Application for Federal Employment, is typed neatly without any errors and reflects your work accomplishments. For private-sector positions you must have a resumé that reflects your experience.

40. Call the personnel office for feedback on your application. If you are notified that someone else has been selected, do not toss your application on the shelf until the next job opening. Call up the personnel office and determine (it is your right to know) where you were weak and ask what were they looking for that you lacked. You may find out that you did not lack the qualifications but you did not write enough about your accomplishments.

41. Rewrite your SF-171 or resumé to take this feedback into account and to incorporate more of your strengths and your objectives. Your quest in this endeavor is to learn what is needed to get your application past the panel into the hands of a selecting official and to the interview stage. When you apply for your next position, you will be ready.

42. Keep applying. This is the way to learn from others.

Assessing Where You Are

43. Evaluate your commitment to your career.

44. Document all your efforts in applying for other positions—the name of the job applied for, the location, and the lessons learned from the experience.

45. Document your successes and your efforts of improvement. Keep a list on how you are doing.

46. Write down your failures and what you learned from them. Celebrate the learning and your growth.

47. Search for other opportunities to learn about vacancies. Call personnel offices directly or visit the OPM. Let others know you are interested in changing jobs. More jobs are found through other people than by applying cold to a job. Sometimes you have to know someone, or they need to know who you are and the type of work that you do.

48. Realistically determine if you need to acquire specific training in a particular area.

49. Plan your next step. Look for meaningful experiences in different work settings.

Reviewing the Lessons

50. Review the 33 lessons and 16 events discussed in Chapters 4 and 5.

51. Determine the lesson you most need to learn.

52. Discover what event(s) taught the specific lesson, and make a plan of action on how you can take advantage of having this event in your own career plan.

53. Describe what you feel comfortable in doing to learn this lesson.

54. Ask your supervisor for the "event" that will help you learn. A carefully planned sequence of job moves enables one to acquire varied skills and ensures levels of success.

55. Sell your supervisor on the benefits to be derived by the organization if you are provided the chance to learn.

56. Complete your action plan that incorporates this lesson into many work areas. For example, the lesson How Government Works, which was rated the most significant lesson that had made a difference, is comprehensive. It provides the foundation by which people learn how the system works; how it functions; the processes that are required for government to work; the projects that are underway; the political environment and its implication on how government serves its constituents; key people to know; and the culture of the organization. Learning how government works can be gained through many sources. The one most cited was bosses and role models.

57. Be open to stretching yourself. Once you have mastered the lesson, make sure you celebrate passing this milestone in your career.

Observing the Boss

58. Realize the importance of a good boss. Bosses teach both positively and negatively. People learn from observing others and emulating them when it fits within their framework and value system.

59. Discover what kind of boss you like: one who gives you autonomy or who micromanages; one who guides you but does not direct you; one from whom you can learn from his or her experiences or one who leaves you to learn on your own?

60. Tell your boss your preferred method of working relationship and what your goals are.

61. Take advantage of this valuable resource. Learn from observation and this person's knowledge.

62. Absorb all the information provided. Store it; you never know when it may be needed.

63. Search for opportunities to show off what you have learned from the boss. Make sure you give him or her credit.

64. Let your boss be aware of how he or she is contributing to your career goals.

Exploring the Culture

65. Learn to recognize the culture of an organization. Is it task oriented or people oriented? Ask which you are. Do your values match or conflict with the culture of the organization? If they conflict, be prepared to take some detours in your career.

66. Recognize the value of the organizational culture and the role it takes in deciding your career movement.

67. Prepare yourself for culture changes, especially in the political context.

68. Indoctrinate yourself in the ins and outs of political relationships and their power.

69. Discover where you are in the culture and where your unit is. What impact does it have in the organizational structure?

70. Explore the many facets of culture.

71. Use your cultural knowledge to bring about change in your favor. Information is power.

72. Focus on your career and how it is part of the culture of the organization. How does it make you feel?

Is It Time for a Mentor?

73. Document what you want to learn from a mentor and what you want that person to do for you.

74. List a number of people whom you admire, and write down why you admire them and what they can do for you.

75. Strategize your options and the best choice for your mentor.

76. List the kind of relationship you want from the mentor.

77. Call for an appointment and visit the person you have selected as a mentor to check out your compatibility.

78. If compatible, ask if the person is willing to be your mentor and if she is willing to draw up a contract on intent of accomplishments. It is very important to have a time line with the mentor to ensure adequate time is spent that is meaningful to both.

79. Validate within yourself that only one mentor is needed.

80. Keep a journal of your meeting along with any decisions that are made with your mentor.

Managing Your Career

81. Review the lessons and events in the light of the new lessons you need to learn.

82. Cover all bases by incorporating into your management portfolio as many learning opportunities as possible.

83. Strive to learn all 33 lessons, and be on familiar terms with the teachers of these lessons.

84. Make the lessons work for you as you manage your career.

85. Seek out opportunities to be visible and productive. Be your own sales and marketing agent.

86. Strategize your next movement up or across the ladder. Know your needs.

87. Visualize your next step by reviewing your accomplishments since you have started on this journey.

Preparing to Make the Jump

88. Be creative and innovative in preparing for the jump.

89. Be known for your honesty, integrity, and getting the job done.

90. Be physically conditioned to make the jump, realizing the average executive works 10- to 14-hour days. Know your energy level.

91. Be more than confident. You have worked all your life on the goal to make it to the top. You know you are mentally, intellectually, and physically ready to meet the challenge.

92. Be alert to opportunities. Use all your resources, talents, skills, and interpersonal relationships to make the right time and the right place happen together.

93. Use resources of others. At this level, others play a direct role in having a voice in who makes it to the top. Select your others wisely.

94. Focus your energies on getting your new executive position.

Making the Jump to the Top

95. Document your successes and what you did that was the crucial advantage to your selection over others.

96. Know your advantage, because this transition—moving from a management to an executive role in the senior executive cadre—is proclaimed to be the hardest to make.

97. Capitalize on your talents and make a good impression.

98. Ask many questions. Become knowledgeable and build from there. Do not change anything at first.

99. Learn to settle in comfortably and establish yourself, preferably within the first three months of the job.

100. Enjoy your new life at the top.

These steps are only a capsule view of a career journey—a journey that takes a lifetime for most. The challenge and excitement of planning and living this journey are all part of adjusting to the executive's job at the top.

NOTES

1. Rensis Likert, *New Patterns of Management* (New York: McGraw-Hill, 1961).

2. Patricia Aburdene and John Naisbitt, *Megatrends for Women* (New York: Villard Books, 1992), 92.

3. John Robinson quoted in Hilton Hotels Corporation, *Time Values Survey* (1991).

4. Abraham H. Maslow, *Motivation and Personality* (New York: Harper & Row, 1954).

Appendix A: Survey Questionnaire

QUESTIONNAIRE FOR SENIOR EXECUTIVES

NAME: (Optional)_____ DATE:_____
AGENCY: _____GRADE: _____ AGE: ___ NO. OF YEARS
IN FEDERAL SERVICE: ___ IN SES: ___ AS GM-15: ___ AS GM-14:___
EDUCATION: Major in School: _____ Highest Degree earned: _____
Attended FEI? Yes ___ No ___

If you would like to be interviewed instead of completing the questionnaire, please call Ms. Danity Little on 301-774-6052.

As a member of the Senior Executive Service, you have attained one of
the highest achievements in the career public service. To assist others in
achieving this honor, the attached questionnaire has been designed to
capture your path to the SES — how, what, and where you learned your
leadership talents. This questionnaire was developed by the Center for
Creative Leadership to address "how executives learn." The purpose of
this research study is to determine how public sector women executives
learn and progress up the career ladder. The secondary purpose is to
replicate the private sector research study in the public sector and to do a
comparative analysis.

If you would like to receive a copy of the compiled research results,
please provide your address below:

INSTRUCTIONS FOR QUESTIONNAIRE

Questions can be answered by bullet points or with complete sentences.
You are encouraged to be as specific as possible in describing your career progression. If you need more space, please use either the reverse
side or additional pages. If you should have any questions, please contact Ms. Danity Little at (301) 774-6052.

Thank you for the time and effort which you have expended in responding
to the questions contained in this survey.

UNIVERSITY OF SOUTHERN CALIFORNIA
Washington Public Affairs Center
512 Tenth Street, N.W.
Washington, D.C., 20004

RESEARCH QUESTIONNAIRE FOR SENIOR EXECUTIVES*

SECTION I

When you think about your career in managing people, certain events or episodes probably stand out in your mind—things that led to a lasting change in your approach to management. Please identify at least three "key events" in your career: things that made a difference in the way you manage now.

By each event describe:

1. What happened?

2. What did you learn from it (for better or worse)?

Please use separate sheets of paper.

SECTION II

Having listed key events that really stood out, we will now address some things that may or may not have had a lasting effect on you. You may comment as lengthy as you wish on the following questions. On the questions that are important to you, please be more specific and provide greater detail.

A. RITES OF PASSAGE

1. What was your "organizational first date"—like your first real date, a time when you were all alone and had to take complete responsibility for something you had never done before?

2. What was the biggest challenge you ever faced?

3. What was your most frightening first—something you did for the first time that really had you worried?

*Permission granted by the Center for Creative Leadership to use and modify the private sector guidelines.

Page 2. Research Questionnaire for Senior Executives

---

4. What event (or events) made you realize you were going to be successful as a manager?

   Did it occur in your current organization?

5. What was your first managerial job?

   What was special about it?

   What do you recall about your first boss?

6. What was your first "quantum leap"—i.e. movement to a job with significantly more responsibility/challenge/pressure than prior jobs?

7. Describe your first important interchanges with and exposure to high-level executives?

   Have there been other interchanges that stand out for you?

B. RISING FROM THE ASHES

1. What was your darkest hour?

2. What was a significant near miss—a time when you tried something and failed?

3. Describe a time when you pushed things to the brink—that is, a time when you stretched the system by coming perilously close to violating rules, norms, or authority.

Page 3. Research Questionnaire for Senior Executives

---

4. What was your most significant act of procrastination? By this we mean a time when you didn't face up to a situation that got steadily worse, resulting in a mess.

5. Do you recall a time when you had the rug pulled out from under you—a situation when you had everything ready to go and the door was slammed shut? Please describe.

6. Were you ever worn out or fed up, but managed to restart? Please describe.

7. Did you ever learn a great truth that turned out to be a falsehood? That is, was there ever a case where you thought you had learned something significant but later found out it wasn't so? Please describe.

8. Recall a situation you took very seriously at the time but were able to laugh about months (or years) later?

C. THE ROLE OF OTHER PEOPLE

1. Please describe the person who taught you the most during your career. What did that person do that made him or her so special?

2. Most of us have worked for a person we simply couldn't tolerate for one reason or another. What did you learn from such an experience?

Page 4. Research Questionnaire for Senior Executives

———————————————————————————————————————

3. What was your most significant interpersonal conflict—a situation in which dealing with another person (or persons) was very difficult for you?

SECTION III: GENERAL QUESTIONS

1. Overall, how have you changed, plus and minus, over your career? If you ran into someone who knew you well years ago, what differences would he or she notice?

2. Describe times when you've been more open to learning than others?

    More closed?

3. What part have events in your personal life played in your growth as a manager?

4. What about being a manager has been fun for you?

    What are some examples of situations or events you particularly enjoyed?

    That were the most fun?

5. What advice would you give to a younger manager about managing his or her career?

    What do you need to do for yourself?

    How much should you let others do for you (or to you)?

Page 5. Research Questionnaire for Senior Executives

———————————————————————————————

6. What is the most significant thing you've learned as an adult—the one thing you would pass on to someone else if you could?

7. What's next?

    Are you facing a situation now from which you expect to learn something new? Yes__ No__ If answer is yes, please describe.

Appendix B: Key Events and Lessons Definitions

KEY EVENTS

ASSIGNMENTS

First Supervisory Job: The first job in which the manager was responsible for the supervision of others. First Supervisory Job assignments welcomed these executives to the world of management and a new realm of problems, i.e., people.

Managing a Larger Scope: An increase in responsibility that was both broader and different from what had gone before. Changes in scope included switching to new [agencies, divisions, locations] and massive increases in numbers of people, dollars, and functions to manage. In scope changes, managers coped with numerous problems: the enormity of the job, pressure from top management, staffing and [budget] problems, and unfamiliarity with the [mission, function, system], etc. [In many cases, a larger scope was the present SES job. This could be staff to line switches, technical to manager, scientist to manager, expert to manager and specialist to generalist.]

In all scope changes, managers were confronted with a new situation in which their knowledge was, in some way, incomplete. [Many of these had been in deputy positions; the person in charge left and they took over. When the boss left, the person had to take over without adequate training.] While directing others and seeing that operations ran smoothly, they had to learn essential parts of their job on the run. Getting their arms around the job was the consistent theme of this event.

Project/Task Force Assignments: Discrete projects or temporary assignments, done alone or as part of a team or task force. Aimed at specific outcomes, they brought deadlines and high visibility. They typically involved grasping new content areas or activities

Excerpted from *Key Events in Executives' Lives*, E. Lindsey, V. Homes, and M. W. McCall, Jr., October 1987, Center for Creative Leadership, Technical Report 32. The bracketed information expands the definitions to incorporate specifics from the federal government.

and grappling with new relationships. These were typically taken on as short-term as-signments rather than as new jobs per se. Often they were extracurricular to a manager's job, creating additional demands on a manager's time.

Whatever the type, durations, or complexity of the assignment, Project/Task Force As-signments were begun to meet a particular organizational goal. More than other assign-ments, these had expected and recognizable endpoints indicated by the failure or success of a project.

Turning [an Organization] Around: Fixing and stabilizing, turning around a failing op-eration was the key to successful completion of this event. Stabilizing operations gone haywire required managers to dismantle and reconstruct existing operations that were blatantly characterized by poor [organizational] performance and, almost always, by re-sistant, demoralized, or incompetent staffs. Due to the need to simultaneously tear down and build up staff and systems, managers were forced to exhibit opposites in their be-havior—toughness and structuring behaviors had to be counterbalanced with persuasion and a light touch.

Although the core problems were fairly clear, these managers usually discovered un-expected problems and obstacles for which they were often unprepared. Restoring long-lost credibility with [departmental] headquarters coupled with high visibility and pressure was often reported in the line environment. Staff position and [project] fixes typically placed managers in situations in which they lacked authority over people (e.g., management, customers) whose support they needed. In addition to these obstacles, some of these managers found themselves in new cultures or [organizational] arenas or as replacements for well-liked managers.

Turning an organization around conditions were sometimes created by reorganiza-tions following [new legislation, turnover in administration] and sometimes discovered by managers upon a transfer or promotion.

Line-to-Staff Switches: These events involved managers who moved (not always by choice) from line operations to [agency] staff roles. The purpose of these assignments was to teach managers the other side of the organization and expose them to agency strategies and culture, but the jobs themselves varied greatly. Unlike many other events, Line-to-Staff Switches do not fall into neat subcategories: The assigned areas encom-passed planning, training, and human resources, and productivity improvement. There was also wide variation in the length of assignment [three-month stint to permanent job] and level of the manager [entry level to special assistant]. [Sometimes these positions were policy writing or interpreting for high-level executives.]

Starting from Scratch: Building something from nothing or from almost nothing. Orga-nizational strategies for growth and expansion were met through such assignments as [opening up a new field office, creating a new department, designing and introducing a new bill and following it through Congress, implementing and enforcing a project or pol-icy, designing new programs, setting up a laboratory, establishing a training center, or set-ting up a new function based upon a reorganization.]

HARDSHIPS

Career Setback: These events are cases of a job-person mismatch, in which something about the manager's position was regarded as a career setback. These managers de-scribed how they had been demoted, exiled to crummy jobs, or had seen a badly wanted promotion given to someone else. The common theme is that the job did not suit perceived skills or aspirations. The circumstances leading up to the setbacks ranged from being in the wrong place during a reorganization, [a political changeover], to personal mistakes. [Some had taken ethical stands and said they would resign before they would do "the project."] Regardless of the nature or cause of these events, troublesome circumstances had occurred or accrued and managers, recognizing an incongruity, felt stuck or stung.

Changing Jobs: Changing jobs is about changing careers. In these events executives traded in successful (or at least known) careers for a chance at something new. [They were "breaking a rut."] Some of these moves were preceded by discontent and accompanied by a willingness to take risks. Some managers insisted on being transferred to new areas while others left [departments] they had been with for over a decade. The tactics varied, but their goals were the same: to find new challenges with continued career growth. [Changing jobs also meant having a variety of job changes, by career, agency, new fields of endeavor, or from private to public positions.]

Personal Trauma: Crisis experiences with a powerful emotional impact. Executives described events in which their families, health, even their lives, were threatened by unanticipated tragedies. These traumas stemmed from both work and personal life and include personal injury or illness, the death of others, divorce, and combat duty.

The consequences of the trauma events were profound and far reaching. Managers were forced to reevaluate aspects of their lives that they had previously taken for granted, and in many cases, the trauma's impact was compounded by other life events. In order to overcome the effects of these hardships, managers often found it necessary to make lasting changes in their behavior and attitudes.

These events and their traumatic effects varied in severity and degree of suddenness, but, regardless of the specific nature of the event, all had a profound and personal impact.

Employee Performance Problems: In these events managers had to confront an employee with a problem that was performance related. The problems revolved around ineptness, alcoholism, drugs, and older managers who had let technology pass them by.

According to these executives, trouble with employees was common in many of their job assignments, but not the focus of the event. When managers recounted subordinate performance problems, the nature of the assignment was rarely mentioned and the context of their jobs was irrelevant. These hardship events were distinguished by the one-on-one confrontation with the problem individual. Managers had to deal with the failure and mistakes of employees while genuinely upset over the pathos of the situation.

Two types of actions were taken in these situations. First, the manager would usually try to salvage the situation through counseling and development. If the subordinate did not respond (or the situation was hopeless), managers were forced to [take steps to remove or transfer] or to fire the person.

[Organizational] Mistakes: Stories of managerial shortcomings that derailed goals. Errors were made in dealing with people critical to a project's success. Failure to give or obtain necessary information, support, or agreement on specific issues curtailed plans and collapsed [organizational projects].

[Organizational] mistakes include ideas that didn't fly, conflicts that got out of hand, deals that fell through, and failures to make the most of opportunities. Although specific outcomes were diverse, these events were united by two themes: The outcomes were unsatisfactory to the manager involved and they stemmed from mistakes in dealing with key people.

OTHER PEOPLE

Bosses/[Role Models]: Superiors that managers interacted with, or observed, during the course of their careers. Some of these models were characterized as possessing exceptional skills or attributes. Others were remembered for their weaknesses and the impact those had on people. But, regardless of whether the role model was positive, negative, or a little of both, each case described a person who profoundly influenced the executive's approach to management.

Values Playing Out: Snapshots of behavior occurring at work. These were short-lived events involving a person (or persons) doing something to another person (or persons) that had a visible impact. The manager, as an actor in the scene or as an observer of it, drew a value-laden conclusion from it. Events of this type almost always were of short duration, occurred in chain-of-command relationships, and were discussed "out of context"—that is, the "snapshot" had survived while the larger scenario in which it happened had dimmed. The values conveyed were primarily what one ought or ought not to do in dealing with other people. [Sometimes willing to take risks for the values involved entered into the picture—budget cuts, space allocations, and RIFs were cited examples.]

OTHER EVENTS

Purely Personal: A range of experiences outside the workplace that contributed to manager's development. The experiences described had occurred in family, school, community: life in general. Their occurrence ranged in time from childhood to the present, and they varied in nature from difficult situations to inspirational ones.

Coursework: The formal training and academic programs attended by managers. [Formal education or intern programs where one is exposed to many high level people, different offices and occupations and functions.] The specific purpose of these events is to provide managers the opportunity to obtain information and experiences not available from their day-to-day jobs. [More than one executive explained they were avid readers and gleaned most of their current knowledge which was important to their position from books, articles, and journals.]

Early Work Experience: Important work experiences that took place early in the managers' careers. In most cases these were non-management jobs that introduced the aspiring manager to new environments, cultures, and management philosophies.

LESSON DEFINITIONS

All about [How Government Works]: Learning about one's area [of expertise in the organization (e.g., operations, research, personnel, financial, law, accounting)] or organizational [structure, financial or budgetary practices, legislative process, systems and processes, politics and constituents].

Balance between Work and Personal Life: Encompasses the kinds of examining, reevaluating and prioritizing that managers experience in balancing their work and personal life. Key within this category is recognizing the values of life outside work and discovering the importance of slowing down and relaxing in one's work life.

Basic Management Values: Statements of ideal values and practices and undesirable practices or management values or principles that guide appropriate, ethical behavior as a manager. Most of the lessons in this category are examples of the integrity, trust, and credibility a manager must exemplify.

Being Tough When Necessary: Developing the strength to do what must be done in the service of the organization, even though it may involve a human cost. Being tough requires the ability to stand fast (resist pressure to back off) and to move ahead (grit one's teeth although the action to be taken has the potential of hurting others). This lesson involves learning that even when an action may hurt someone, to procrastinate is harmful. [Hold people accountable for their work].

Building and Using Structure and Control Systems: Learning to manage without being involved in every phase of day-to-day operations by setting up structures and systems which control work processes, building and controlling systems so they can run without the manager; changing structure rather than people allows managing by remote control.

Confronting Employee Performance Problems: Learning that it's more important to make the move quickly, and at the same time making sure one has adequate staffing to pick up the slack if the decision is a move to terminate. [Confronting people about their performance throughout the year not just at evaluation time helped managers take action quickly.]

Coping with Ambiguous Situations: Discovering that one has the capacity to manage in an ambiguous situation. This category includes two major kinds of learnings: that even with incomplete knowledge one has the ability to act in a turbulent context, putting out brush fires while learning the job; and that learning on the run is one way to learn new skills while using old ones. [Learning to be flexible in an unstructured and uncertain environment; remaining flexible.]

Coping with Situations beyond Your Control: The recognition that there are times when one faces a situation that one can do nothing to change; that some situations are influenced by factors outside of the manager's control such as luck, others' performance, and unrealistic expectations. Coping with such situations requires ways of dealing with or making the best of the uncontrollable situations by changing goals, being patient or optimistic, distancing oneself, or redefining the situations. [Fate and timing play a role.]

Dealing with Conflict: Recognizing and learning that conflict is endemic; that one can deal with conflict or learn to deal with it by reducing, resolving, or avoiding it. [Personal conflict represented by different management styles.]

Dealing with People over Whom You Have No Authority: Getting cooperation in non-authority relationships, lateral relationships and others. Overall, this category states that to get things done one must be able to involve many others over whom one has no direct authority or control. [Learned to compromise and negotiate working with others.]

Developing Other People: Learning that part of dealing with employees is developing them. This includes understanding that people can be helped to change and learn if the "right" environment (challenges, opportunity) is provided, and that individual growth benefits the organization. [Provide people training and opportunities to grow.]

Directing and Motivating Employees: The staffing, managing, and directing required in building a working organization. Delegation, sharing responsibility, building competence, team building, and leadership roles are predominate topics. [Giving feedback and recognizing people.]

Getting People to Implement Solutions: Learning how to get people to implement solutions in terms of both requirements and challenges entails a shift in focus from individual task performance to managing people in order to accomplish a task. This category contains the recognition that people are key, that they can contribute either to accomplishments or to roadblocks. It also contains the realization that management requires reliance on and working through others. [Management is different from technical; people are important.]

Handling Political Situations: Encompasses both the realization that organizations are, in part, political systems and recommendations for dealing within them. For example, a recognition of the political component in decision making may result in the discovery that one needs to make a personal choice regarding the use of politics to achieve a goal—to sell a point, idea, or project.

How to Work with Executives: How to work with executives in various contexts, from how to present ideas to them to the importance of impressing and not antagonizing them. This category contains critical deportment skills and the art of cajoling. [Giving presentations, making briefings, and associating with high-level executives.]

Innovative Problem-Solving Methods: Lessons in the art of problem solving, in transcending habitual ways of thinking about problems. [Includes being a risk taker.]

Knowing What Really Excites You about Work: Coming to the realization that one has found something which is exciting and worth doing on its own merit. This something can be a subject area, working with others, a lifestyle, or a contribution to something larger than one's self.

Management Models: Formal management theories or processes learned [on the job or through coursework] during the course of a career.

Managing Former Bosses and Peers: Lessons that managers learn as they begin to be promoted over their peers and bosses and must deal with them in a different role. Stressed are the importance of light-handedness and knowing that one can neither make everyone happy nor always win.

Persevering through Adversity: Developing ways to accomplish one's goals in the face of obstacles, recognizing that difficult situations are often not out of one's control, and acting on them. [Worked more than 10 hours a day and weekends; committed to the job; used to hard work, persevered, took risks, resilient and purposeful. Surviving when people are out to "get you" or on the "political out."]

Personal Limits and Blind Spots: Coming to terms with personal limits and blind spots in managing, that often stem from lack of time and/or lack of expertise to accomplish alone the variety of tasks necessary to be successful.

Recognizing and Seizing Opportunities: The notion that much of what happens is serendipitous; that one must be prepared to take advantage of opportunities as they arise. Examples are: seize opportunities, prepare for the unexpected, don't assume time/opportunities are unlimited, plan ahead, develop a second skill.

Self-Confidence: Statements of self-trust, knowing oneself, and arrogance. They span trust in one's own competence, in one's ability to take risks, handle tough situations, and be successful.

Sensitivity to the Human Side of Management: Fundamental assumptions of one's value about human beings. This category contains statements of warmth and caring and of insights into human nature. The fact that people are the [organization] and have needs and lives which go beyond the day-to-day functions they perform lends awareness to the importance of sensitivity to others. In this category fall insights into how people should be treated and why. [Be fair to people and put yourself in other people's shoes.]

Shouldering Full Responsibility: Taking full responsibility, assuming the risk for the group.

Strategic Thinking: Learning to rise above day-to-day operations, to take a [departmental] view, and gain a broader perspective. This represents the transition from a short-term, smaller-scope view of the organization to being able to look at the big picture, seeing both a longer time frame and a broader organizational scope. Developing a longer time frame/strategic perspective involves looking at the [department] as a whole, thinking about its mission and direction. Seeing a broader organizational scope also involves looking at the organization with respect to its environment, legislation, and international issues. [It also contributes to national well-being.]

Strategies of Negotiation: Learning to deal with various types of external groups (i.e., clients, [state, local, and other] governments, [Congress, White House, Office of Management and Budget, academia, unions, scientific communities, public, press, industries, and private businesses]) in situations involving formal negotiation. These include adversarial, collaborative and customer/client relationships. [Different tactics were required for each group, especially winning favor with Congress.]

Taking Charge of Your Career: Variations on the theme of how to take charge of the situation one is currently in; for example, realizing that you are the only one who can manage your career, set your own pace, broaden it if it gets too easy, set goals, and go.

Technical/Professional Skills: Statements of new content in a well-defined technical area. This category includes learning technical or [specialty] content areas such as finance, strategic planning, personnel, computers, budgeting, engineering, science, medicine, and law. [Includes being an expert in the field and recognized for your skill in this specialty area. Other skills noted could be in writing and speaking.]

Understanding Other People's Perspectives: Dealing with people other than one's peers, bosses, and subordinates requires understanding their perspectives, speaking their language. These languages emphasize the notion that people are different and that to be successful in dealing or communicating with them, one must be sensitive to these differences and act in accordance. [Includes understanding people's work jargon, i.e., language of engineer different from that of personnel. Also be empathetic and aware of different cultures.]

Use and Abuse of Power: Examples of dealing with the double-edged sword of power. Inherent within this category is recognition of the dilemma that use of power may either help or hinder the attainment of desired ends. [Includes the power of "taking charge," giving orders, and making decisions.]

What Executives Are Like: Learning what executives are like, both the positives and the negatives, demystifies the executive aura. This category describes executives as human beings and describes what they value, how they operate, and how they see things. [It comes from working with high-level executives early in their career and frequently being involved in activities with high-level executives.]

You Can't Manage Everything All Alone: The discovery that, by its very nature, the managerial job cannot be done alone; that delegation and reliance on others are crucial components of the job; realizing that the scope is too large to handle alone; that one's managerial success requires [persuasive negotiating skills], building teams; and relationships and reliance on others.

Selected Bibliography

Andrews, Lynn V. *Windhorse Woman*. New York: Warner Books, 1989.

Barnard, C. *The Functions of the Executive: Thirtieth Anniversary Edition*. Cambridge: Harvard University Press, 1968.

Bass, B. M. *Leadership and Performance beyond Expectations*. New York: Free Press, 1986.

Beitz, Charles A., Jr. "A Case Study in Applying Adult Learning Theory and Assessment Center Technology in Developing Senior Leaders." D.P.A. diss., University of Southern California, 1986.

Benne, Kenneth D., Leland P. Bradford, Jack R. Gibb, and Ronald O. Lippitt, eds. *The Laboratory Method of Changing and Learning Theory and Application*. Palo Alto, CA: Science and Behavior Books, 1975.

Bennis, W., and Nanus, B. *Leaders: The Strategies for Taking Charge*. New York: Harper & Row, 1985.

Bern, Paula R. *How to Work for a Woman Boss Even If You'd Rather Not*. New York: Dodd, Mead, 1987.

Bogdan, R. C., and S. K. Biklen. *Qualitative Research for Education*. Boston: Allyn and Bacon, 1982.

Bogue, E. G. *The Enemies of Leadership: Lessons for Leaders in Education*. Bloomington, IN: Phi Delta Kappa Educational Foundation, 1985.

Bok, Derek. "Report of the Task Force on Education and Training to the National Commission on the Public Service." In *Investment for Leadership: Education and Training for the Public Service*. Washington, DC: Task Force on Education and Training, 1989.

Brookfield, Stephen D. *Understanding and Facilitating Adult Learning*. San Francisco: Jossey-Bass, 1986.

Brothers, Joyce. *The Successful Woman*. New York: Simon and Schuster, 1988.

Bruce, J. S. *The Intuitive Pragmatists: Conversations with Chief Executive Officers*. Greensboro, NC: Center for Creative Leadership, 1986.

Bryan, Alan. *Leadership and Organizations*. London: Routledge and Kegan Paul, 1986.

Burns, J. M. *Leadership*. New York: Harper & Row, 1978.

Calkin, Homer L. *Women in the Department of State: Their Role in American Foreign Affairs*. Department of State Publication 8951. Washington, DC: U.S. Government Printing Office, 1978.

Campbell, C. *Managing the Presidency: Carter, Reagan, and the Search for Executive Harmony*. Pittsburgh, PA: University of Pittsburgh Press, 1986.

Carnevale, Anthony P., and Leila J. Gainer. *The Learning Experience*. Washington, DC: American Society for Training and Development and U.S. Department of Labor, [1989].

Carnevale, Anthony P., Leila J. Gainer, and Ann S. Meltzer. *Workplace Basics: The Skills Employers Want*. Washington, DC: American Society for Training and Development and U.S. Department of Labor, [1988].

Carulli, Lorraine M., Cheryl Li Noroian, and Andy Levine. "Employee-Driven Career Development." *Personnel Administrator* 34 (March 1989): 87–90.

Clark, Kenneth E., and Miriam B. Clark, eds. *Measures of Leadership*. West Orange, NJ: Leadership Library of America, 1990.

Clark, Miriam B., and Frank H. Freeman, eds. *Leadership Education 1990: A Source Book*. Greensboro, NC: Center for Creative Leadership, and West Orange, NJ: Leadership Library of America, 1990.

Clemens, J. K., and D. F. Mayer. *The Classic Touch: Lessons in Leadership from Homer to Hemingway*. Homewood, IL: Dow Jones–Irwin, 1987.

Cleveland, H. *The Knowledge Executive: Leadership in an Information Society*. New York: Dutton, 1985.

Cohen, M. D., and J. G. March. *Leadership and Ambiguity*. 2d ed. Boston: Harvard Business School Press, 1986.

Cohen, Sherry Suib. *Tender Power*. Reading, MA: Addison-Wesley, 1988.

Cornwall-Jones, A. T. *Education for Leadership: The International Administrative Staff Colleges, 1948–1984*. Boston: Routledge and Kegan Paul, 1985.

Culbert, Samuel A., and Warren H. Schmidt. "Staging a Behavioral Science Learning Experience: Transforming Observers into Participants." *Journal of Applied Behavioral Science* 5 (1969): 337–349.

Dill, William R., Wallace B. S. Crowston, and Edwin J. Elton. "Strategies for Self-Education." *Harvard Business Review* 46 (November–December 1965): 119–130.

Doig, J. W. *Leadership and Innovation: A Biographical Perspective on Entrepreneurs in Government*. Baltimore: Johns Hopkins University Press, 1987.

Donnell, Susan M., and Jay Hall. "Men and Women as Managers: A Significant Case of No Significant Difference." *Organizational Dynamics* 8 (Spring 1980): 50–77.

Douglas, Emily Taft. *Remember the Ladies*. New York: G. P. Putnam's Sons, 1966.

Drucker, Peter F. *The Changing World of the Executive*. New York: Times Books, 1982.

———. *The Practice of Management*. New York: Harper & Row, 1986.

Duffey, Joseph. "Competitiveness and Human Resources." *California Management Review* 30 (Spring 1988): 92–100.

Dye, T. R. *Who's Running America? The Conservative Years*. 4th ed. Englewood Cliffs, NJ: Prentice-Hall, 1986.

Fiedler, F. E. *A Theory of Leadership Effectiveness*. New York: McGraw-Hill, 1967.

Fiedler, F. E., and M. M. Chemers. *Leadership Style and Effective Management*. Glenview, IL: Scott, Foresman, 1974.

Fierman, Jaclyn. "Why Women Still Don't Hit the Top." *Fortune*, July 30, 1990, 40–62.

Flanders, Loretta R. "Qualifications and Competence." *The Bureaucrat* (Spring 1983): 48–50.

Flynn, Patricia M. *Facilitating Technological Change: The Human Resource Challenge.* Cambridge, MA: Ballinger Publishing, 1988.

Friedman, Thomas. *Up the Ladder: Coping with the Corporate Climb.* New York: Warner Books, 1986.

Frost, P. J., V. V. Mitchell, and W. R. Nord. *Organizational Reality—Reports from the Firing Line.* 3d ed. Glenview, IL: Scott, Foresman, 1986.

Gazda, George M., Frank S. Asbury, Fred J. Balzer, William C. Childers, and Richard P. Walters. *Human Relations Development: A Manual for Educators.* 3d ed. Newton, MA: Allyn and Bacon, 1984.

Greenleaf, R. K. *Servant Leadership: A Journey into the Nature of Legitimate Power and Greatness.* New York: Paulist Press, 1977.

Guba, E. G., and Y. S. Lincoln. *Effective Evaluation.* San Francisco: Jossey-Bass Publishers, 1982.

Guest, R. H., P. Hersey, and K. Blanchard. *Organizational Change through Effective Leadership.* 2d ed. Englewood Cliffs, NJ: Prentice-Hall, 1986.

Hambrick, Donald C., and Phyllis A. Mason. "Upper Echelons: The Organization as a Reflection of Its Top Managers." *Academy of Management Review* 9 (1984): 193–206.

Hart, Lois Borland. *Moving Up.* New York: AMACOM, 1980.

Hastings, Anne H., and Larry S. Beyna. "Woman and Career Advancement: Experiences from within the Department of Health and Human Services." Report submitted to Office of the Assistant Secretary for Personnel Administration, U.S. Department of Health and Human Services. Arlington, VA: Scanlon & Hastings, 1985.

Hein, E. C. *Contemporary Leadership Behavior: Selected Readings.* 2d ed. Boston: Little, Brown, 1986.

Heller, T. *Leaders and Followers: Challenges for the Future.* Greenwich, CT: JAI Press, 1986.

Herren, Laura M. "The Right Recruitment Technology for the 1990's." *Personnel Administrator* 34 (April 1989): 48–52.

Hersey, P. *The Situational Leader: The Other 59 Minutes.* New York: Warner Books, 1985.

Hersey, P., and K. Blanchard. *Management of Organizational Behavior: Utilizing Human Resources.* 4th ed. Englewood Cliffs, NJ: Prentice-Hall, 1982.

Hewlett, Sylvia Ann. *A Lesser Life.* New York: William Morrow and Company, 1986.

Hodgkinson, C. *The Philosophy of Leadership.* New York: St. Martin's Press, 1983.

Hoferek, M. J. *Going Forth: Woman's Leadership Issues for Women in Higher Education and Physical Education.* Princeton, NJ: Princeton Book Co., 1986.

Honey, Peter, and Alan Mumford. *Capitalizing on Your Learning Opportunities.* King of Prussia, PA: Organization Design and Development, 1990.

———. *Learning Diagnostic Questionnaire Trainer Guide.* Originally published as *The Manual of Learning Opportunities.* Berkshire, England: Ardingly House, 1989; King of Prussia, PA: Organization Design and Development, 1990.

Hutchings, Pat, and Allen Wuitzdorff, eds. *Knowing and Doing: Learning through Experience.* New Directions for Teaching and Learning Series, No. 35. San Francisco: Jossey-Bass, 1988.

Johnston, J. S., Jr. *Educating Managers: Executive Effectiveness through Liberal Learning.* San Francisco: Jossey-Bass, 1986.

Jones, B. D., L. W. Bachelor, and C. Wilson. *The Sustaining Hand: Community Leadership*. Lawrence: University Press of Kansas, 1986.

———. *The Change Masters: Innovation for Productivity in the American Corporation*. New York: Simon & Schuster, 1982.

Kaplan, R. E., W. H. Drath, and J. R. Kofodimos. *High Hurdles, the Challenge of Executive Self-Development*. Technical Report No. 25. Greensboro, NC: Center for Creative Leadership, 1985.

Keirsey, David, and Marilyn Bates. *Please Understand Me: Character and Temperament Types*. 3d ed. Del Mar, CA: Prometheus Nemesis Books, 1978.

Kellerman, B., ed. *Political Leadership*. Pittsburgh, PA: University of Pittsburgh Press, 1986.

———. *Leadership: Multidisciplinary Perspectives*. Englewood Cliffs, NJ: Prentice-Hall, 1984.

Kennedy, D. M., and M. E. Parrish, eds. *Power and Responsibility: Case Studies*. San Diego: Harcourt Brace Jovanovich, 1986.

Kirkpatrick, Donald L. "Supervisory and Management Development: Update from an Expert." *Training and Development Journal* 42 (August 1988): 59–62.

———. *Self-Directed Learning: A Guide for Learners and Teachers*. New York: Associated Press, 1975.

Kotter, J. P. *The Leadership Factor*. New York: Free Press, 1988.

———. *The General Managers*. New York: Free Press, 1982.

Kouzes, J. M., and B. Z. Posner. *The Leadership Challenge*. San Francisco: Jossey-Bass, 1987.

Levinson, H., and S. Rosenthal. *CEO: Corporate Leadership in Action*. New York: Basic Books, 1984.

Lombardo, M. M. *Looking at Leadership: Some Neglected Issues*. Technical Report No. 6. Greensboro, NC: Center for Creative Leadership, 1978.

Losoncy, L. *The Motivating Leader*. Englewood Cliffs, NJ: Prentice-Hall, 1985.

McCall, M. W., Jr., and M. M. Lombardo, eds. *Leadership: Where Else Can We Go?* Durham, NC: Duke University Press, 1978.

Maccoby, M. *The Leader: A New Face for American Management*. New York: Ballantine, 1981.

———. *The Gamesman: The New Corporate Leaders*. New York: Simon & Schuster, 1976.

McGregor, D. M. "An Analysis of Leadership." *Classic Readings in Organizational Behavior*. Edited by J. Stephen Ott. Belmont, CA: Wadsworth, 1989.

Mintzberg, H. *Mintzberg on Management: Inside Our Strange World of Organizations*. New York: Free Press, 1989.

———. *The Nature of Managerial Work*. New York: Harper & Row, 1973.

National Commission on Excellence in Educational Administration. *Leaders for America's Schools*. Tempe, AZ: University Council for Educational Administration, 1987.

Neustadt, R. E., and E. R. May. *Thinking in Time*. New York: Free Press, 1986.

Nodell, Bobbi. "Women in Government." *Government Executive* 20, no. 8 (August 1988): 10–20, 57.

O'Sullivan, Elizabethann, and Gary R. Rassel. *Research Methods for Public Administrators*. New York: Longman, 1989.

Palmer, Albert B. "Learning Cycles: Models of Behavioral Change." In *The 1981 Annual Handbook for Group Facilitators*. Washington, DC: University Associates, 147–151.

Portnoy, R. A. *Leadership: What Every Leader Should Know about People*. Englewood Cliffs, NJ: Prentice-Hall, 1986.

Posner, Barry Z., and Warren H. Schmidt. "Government Morale and Management: A Survey of Federal Executives." *Public Personnel Management* 17 (Spring 1988): 21–27.

Powers, Edward A. "The AMA Management Competency Programs: A Development Process." *EXCHANGE: The Organizational Behavior Teaching Journal* 8 (1983): 16–20.

Sargent, Alice. *The Androgynous Manager*. New York: American Management Association, 1983.

Sayles, Leonard R. *Managerial Behavior*. New York: McGraw-Hill, 1964.

Schaller, L. E. *Getting Things Done: Concepts and Skills for Leaders*. Nashville, TN: Abingdon Press, 1986.

Schmidt, Warren H. "Transforming Knowledge into Impact." Presentation given at the ASTD National Conference, May 14, 1969.

Seeman, Howard. "Why the Resistance to Experiential Learning?" *Education Digest* 54 (December 1988): 28–30.

Selznick, P. *Leadership in Administration: A Sociological Interpretation*. Berkeley: University of California Press, 1983; New York: Harper & Row, 1957.

Sergiovanni, T. J. "Leadership as Cultural Expression." In *Classic Readings in Organizational Behavior*. Edited by J. Stephen Ott. Belmont, CA: Wadsworth, 1989.

Shinn, G. *Leadership Development*. 2d ed. New York: McGraw-Hill, 1986.

Simonton, D. K. *Why Presidents Succeed: A Political Psychology of Leadership*. New Haven, CT: Yale University Press, 1987.

Simosko, Susan. "Assessing Experiential Learning." In *Assessing Students' Learning*. Edited by J. H. Macmillan. San Francisco: Jossey-Bass, 1988.

Smith, Robert M. *Learning How to Learn*. Chicago: Follett Publishing Company, 1982.

Starling, Grover. *Managing the Public Sector*. 3d ed. Chicago: Dorsey Press, 1986.

Stineman, Esther. *Women's Studies: A Recommended Core Bibliography*. Littleton, CO: Libraries Unlimited, 1979.

Stogdill, R. M., and B. M. Bass. *Stogdill's Handbook of Leadership: A Survey of Theory and Research*. New York: Free Press, 1981.

Tannen, Deborah. *You Just Don't Understand: Women and Men in Conversation*. New York: William Morrow and Company, 1990.

Thompson, Ann McKay, and Marcia Donnan Wood. *Management Strategies for Women*. New York: Simon and Schuster, 1980.

Thompson, K. W., ed. *Essays on Leadership: Comparative Insights*. Lanham, MD: University Press of America, 1985.

Tichy, Noel. *Transformational Leader*. New York: Wiley, 1986.

Ulrich, David, and Arthur Young. "A Shared Mindset." *Personnel Administrator* 34 (March 1989): 38–45.

U.S. Civil Service Commission. *Biography of an Ideal: A History of the Federal Civil Service*. Washington, DC: U.S. Government Printing Office, 1976.

U.S. General Accounting Office. "Senior Executive Service Executives' Perspectives on their Federal Service." GAO/GGD-SS-109FS. July 1988.

———. "Senior Executive Service: Reasons the Candidate Development Program Has Not Produced More SES Appointees." GAO/GGD-88-47. April 1988.

Van Fleet, D. D., and G. A. Yukl. *Military Leadership: An Organizational Behavior Perspective*. Greenwich, CT: JAI Press, 1986.

Verlander, Edward G. "Executive Transformation Programs." *Training and Development Journal* 41 (December 1988): 32–35.

Wall, J. A. *Bosses*. Lexington, MA: Lexington Books, 1986.

Wildavsky, A. *The Nursing Father: Moses as a Political Leader*. University: University of Alabama Press, 1984.

Willner, A. R. *The Spellbinders: Charismatic Political Leadership—A Theory*. New Haven, CT: Yale University Press, 1984.

Wilson, Edward O. *On Human Nature*. Cambridge: Harvard University Press, 1978.

"Women: The Road Ahead." Special Issue. *Time*, Fall 1990.

Index

About The Author

DANITY LITTLE is Manager of the International Customs School, U.S. Customs Service, Department of Treasury.